W9-BUV-456

the PALEO SLOW COOKER

the PALEO SLOW COOKER

HEALTHY, GLUTEN-FREE MEALS THE *easy* WAY

Arsy Vartanian
Founder & Chef of rubiesandradishes.com
with Amy Kubal, Registered Dietitian

Foreword by Chris Kresser, L.Ac

Race Point
PUBLISHING

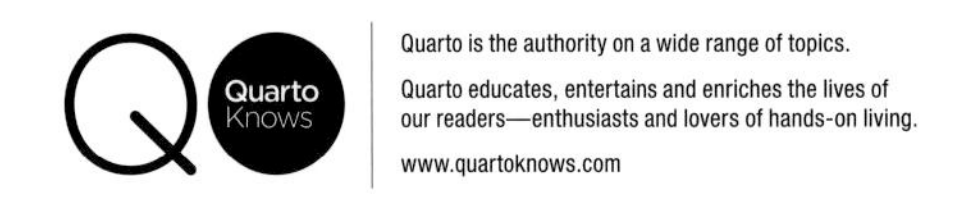

A division of Quarto Publishing Group USA Inc.
142 West 36th Street, 4th Floor
New York, NY 10018
quartoknows.com
Visit our blogs at quartoknows.com

This 2013 edition published by Race Point Publishing by arrangement with Page Street Publishing Co.

ISBN-13: 978-1-63106-311-4

Photography by Tamara Lee Sang
Photograph page 151 © James Baigrie/FoodPix/Getty Images

Printed in China

4 6 8 10 9 7 5 3 2

To my husband, Brooke
my daughter, Indyanna
my parents, Eda & Hayrik
my brothers, Arbi and Aren
and
in memory of my aunt, Valentine

Thank you for the overwhelming love and support.

CONTENTS

FOREWORD BY **CHRIS KRESSER**

I'm different than some of the other contributors in the burgeoning Paleo community because I work with patients on a one-on-one basis. I see clients with a variety of different health concerns, ranging from difficulty losing weight to more serious health problems. This is how I met Arsy a couple of years ago.

Achieving optimal health can be complex, often requiring a variety of lifestyle changes, ranging from sleep to stress management. However, eating real food that will nourish your body is a great starting point. When I took Arsy on as a patient, she had already removed many of the toxins from her diet and her health was beginning to improve significantly as a result. But she was still experiencing some symptoms, such as headaches and lethargy. I worked with her to change her diet even further, emphasizing nutrient-dense foods like bone broth on a regular basis. Arsy was one of my star patients and her story underscores the power of eating a diet void of toxins and rich in nutrients, such as the Paleo diet. And as she mentions in this book, this worked wonders for her. She no longer has headaches and is feeling better than ever. This book reflects the knowledge Arsy has gained by experimenting with her diet to achieve optimal health. Slow cooking became a tool that she utilized often to help her stay committed to these changes, while balancing her busy schedule.

When people are confronted with the concept of following this whole foods approach, they may be hesitant to make the necessary changes thinking that it will require gourmet cooking daily. In reality, many of us do not have the time or money to cook three elaborate meals a day. That is why this book is so necessary. The key to Arsy's success with the Paleo diet has been her interest and skills as a cook and in this book she offers us a way to prepare delicious and healthy meals in a simple and affordable way. Furthermore, this book demonstrates that the Paleo diet does not have to be boring. Arsy brings her Middle-Eastern background with several Armenian and Persian recipes, as well as other ethnic recipes that she has learned about from friends, proving that with the elimination of grains, legumes and dairy, boundless amounts of options still exist.

I have mentioned elsewhere that I prefer the term Paleo Template to Paleo diet, as no single diet is optimal for all individuals. This book does an excellent job of offering recipes that help those with a more individualized approach, from low-carbers to endurance athletes. There are also recipes that are safe for those following an autoimmune protocol. It also includes many recipes using nutritious foods. Animal products, particularly organ meats, are some of the real super foods, but can also be some of the most time-consuming and intimidating to prepare. There are several recipes such as oxtail soup and liver and onions that are valuable for Paleo newbies and seasoned vets alike looking to add more vitamins and minerals into their diet.

I often use a slow cooker myself, and one of my favorite slow-cooked meals is pot roast. It's easy, tastes great and makes enough so that during the week we can open the fridge, heat it up and have a delicious gourmet Paleo meal ready in a few minutes. The slow cooker does a great job of preserving the moisture, tenderness and flavor of a great meal. I will be using this book often to prepare some new healthy dishes.

Most people who switch to a Paleo diet, like Arsy, see significant benefits immediately. They have more energy. They lose weight effortlessly. Many people report increased virility and fertility. Athletes often break their own records. It improves and stabilizes your mood. Many people who were taking anti depressant medications have been able to lower their doses or get off the drugs completely. It also helps people reconnect with their food and food sources, simultaneously strengthening relationships with local farmers and helping people understand just how important food is to our everyday life.

So if you're wondering why I believe in the Paleo diet, it is because I have seen it work in my practice time and time again to reduce inflammation, regulate the immune system and super-charge metabolism by nourishing our bodies with healthy food we crave and need. This book will be a great resource to help you change your eating habits for the better and to stay committed.

—**CHRIS KRESSER**, chriskresser.com, Medicine for the 21st Century

INTRODUCTION

MY TAKE ON THE PALEO DIET

"Ten thousand years ago the Agricultural Revolution was the beginning of a drastic change in the human diet that continues to this day. Today more than 70% of our dietary calories come from foods that our Paleolithic ancestors rarely, if ever, ate. The result is epidemic levels of cardiovascular disease, cancer, diabetes, osteoporosis, arthritis, gastrointestinal disease, and more."

- Dr. Loren Cordain

When I first read *The Paleo Diet* by Dr. Loren Cordain back in 2008, the above quote immediately resonated with me. A lightbulb went off in my head, and I began to understand my own health problems, as well the issues that those around me were experiencing. From that moment on, I could not read enough books, blogs and articles. This is my take on the Paleo diet as a result of everything I have read and experimented with over the past four years.

WHAT IS THE PALEO DIET AND HOW DO YOU FOLLOW IT?

It's a lifestyle that aspires to achieve optimal health by following a diet based on what and how our Paleolithic ancestors ate. The current Paleo movement uses our ancestors as a starting point, but leverages modern science to expand from there. Essentially, it is a diet focused on consuming whole, natural foods, such as meats, eggs, vegetables, fruits, nuts and healthy fats.

How to get started: Eat plenty of meats, seafood, vegetables, eggs, healthy fats and some fruit and nuts. Eliminate the top three food toxins - gluten, industrial/vegetable oils and sugar!

Always purchase the highest-quality ingredients that you can afford. Foods that are organic and grass-fed are not only void of pesticides and antibiotics but are also highly nutritious.

Avoid grains and legumes: It's especially important to avoid wheat and other gluten-containing grains, such as rye and barley. But also avoid soy, corn, beans, and peanuts (they are actually a legume, not a nut).

Avoid added sugars: This includes artificial sweeteners. Only occasionally consume natural sweeteners, such as honey and maple syrup.

Avoid vegetable oils and other processed oils: This includes canola, corn, soybean, cottonseed oil, among others. If you are confused about which fats and oils to consume, check out my "Guide to Using Fats & Oils" on page 14.

Don't be afraid to include healthy fats in your diet: This includes animal fats, avocado, olive oil, coconut oil, palm oil, ghee, grass-fed butter, lard and tallow, among others.

Eat foods with minimal ingredients: If you don't recognize something in the ingredients list or if it is something your grandma didn't eat, chances are neither should you.

Typically a Paleo diet does not include dairy, only consume dairy if you digest it well. If you are not sure how well you tolerate dairy, I suggest cutting it out for a month and then reintroducing it. If you are going to include dairy, it is best to use high-quality dairy from grass-fed sources. Grass-fed dairy is richer in nutrients and has a better fat composition, plus it tastes amazing! The only dairy foods I personally include regularly in my diet are raw milk, heavy cream, grass-fed butter and ghee. However, I will indulge in some high-quality cheese on occasion.

Is the paleo diet a low-carb diet? No, because you can eat certain carbs like yams. There are people who choose to take a low-carb approach, particularly if weight loss is the goal. Depending on your needs, you can adjust accordingly. Athletes may choose to include more starchy options such as sweet potatoes, potatoes, tubers, plantains and bananas.

WHAT ARE SOME OF THE BENEFITS OF THE PALEO DIET?

- Weight loss
- Omega-3/Omega-6 balance in the diet
- Reduced inflammation
- Reduced risk of modern-day diseases such as diabetes, osteoporosis, cancer, heart disease
- Increased energy and focus
- Better athletic performance

SOME TIPS FOR FOLLOWING A PALEO DIET

Clean out your fridge and pantry: Throw out all the foods that you will not be consuming on the Paleo diet.

Eat enough food. Eat until you are full. This may seem counter intuitive because we have been told so often to eat smaller portions. However, when we are eating the foods our bodies were designed to eat, our bodies also know when they have had enough. Trust your body. The Paleo diet typically has a much lighter caloric load than grain-based diets, so you may need to eat more in volume to stay full. If you eat larger meals, you will also need fewer snacks. Snack foods even on a Paleo diet are the ones that are easy to overeat, such as nuts and fruits.

Be very strict the first 2 weeks: Do not "cheat" at all in the first phase. I have found from my own experience and from talking to friends that the first two weeks are the most difficult. You may not feel great at this time because your body is adjusting to the changes in your diet. You may still be craving the foods you used to eat. Stick with it. It will become much easier after this point. I promise!

Be prepared: Preparation is key, especially when you are first starting out. Plan what you are going to eat in advance and prepare whatever you can ahead of time.

I tend to focus on preparing meat in advance, as I find this to be the most time consuming, hence my obsession with the slow cooker. I make a large roast every Sunday and this lasts us for a few meals. This way at dinner time, we can throw together a well-balanced meal quickly.

As the typical American diet is heavily made up of grains, at first glance it seems overwhelming to exclude these foods. As we look at what we can eat, we see that the options are endless on the Paleo Diet. You can have meats, seafood, fruits, vegetables, nuts/seeds, herbs/spices, and healthy sources of fat. Any combination of these foods makes for a fantastic meal!

WHY THE SLOW COOKER?

The slow cooker has many benefits. What initially drew me to it was its convenience. The slow cooker has been my biggest ally in keeping my Paleo diet. I work a day job that requires much commitment and I have a 2-3 hour-a-day commute. Between the hours spent at work, and time with friends and family, I knew that as much as I loved cooking, I could not cook a meal from scratch every night. I also knew that I could not go back to making a quick sandwich for dinner either. I loved how I felt when I ate Paleo-friendly food and wanted a way to continue it. I found the key to my success with the Paleo diet was cooking meat in bulk. When we got home from work, we could just heat it up along with some veggies and have a quick and healthy meal. Then we could spend our evenings enjoying a healthy dinner and catching up about our day!

Besides convenience, the slow cooker is also economical. I know that grass-fed beef can get pricey, especially premium cuts. The slow cooker is a great way to cook inexpensive cuts of meat that tend to be tough but flavorful. The slow-cooking process allows these tough cuts of meat to become tender, juicy and flavorful.

Also it's healthy. And since the food is being cooked at a very low temperature, we never have an opportunity to scorch it and sacrifice the integrity of the ingredients.

SOME SLOW COOKER TIPS

Liquid does not evaporate in the slow cooker, raising the risks of ending up with a bland, watery dish. It requires using flavorful bases, and using more herbs and spices than in conventional cooking. Adding herbs and spices again toward the end of cooking time also helps with flavor.

Browning, although you don't have to do this step if you are busy, really helps to add flavor to your dish!

Also salt tends to dissipate, especially as the vegetables give up liquid. We recommend salting your dishes well at the end to make sure they taste their best.

Sometimes you can end up with quite a bit of liquid when slow cooking. The best thing to do is remove the meat and vegetables when they are done and place the liquid in a sauce pan. Heat over medium heat until you see the sauce thicken, about 5 to 10 minutes. This will also help to concentrate the flavors. Salt after this process so you don't get too much when the liquid evaporates.

You can even make liquids in your slow cooker like homemade broth and coconut milk, both of which are ingredients in the recipes provided throughout the book. I try to avoid canned products whenever I can, so I've provided homemade recipes for these liquids in Chapter 10 (page 234).

FAT IS "WHERE IT'S AT"!

Fat: Artery clogging, heart disease causing, and obesity stimulating—all around BAD stuff. Whoa, wait a minute, that's not right. However, it is unfortunately what the health, medical and food industry have led us to believe. The message that "fat is bad" has been pushed on society for decades. There are "fat-free" and "low-fat" versions of nearly every food and sadly, people are buying them. The truth of the matter is that fat is essential to life and good for us! Now, we're not talking about Crisco, vegetable oils and margarine, but rather natural fats found in grass-fed meats, butter, coconut products, and olive oil.

WHY FAT IS GOOD AND WHAT IT DOES:

Fat provides linoleic and linolenic acid to the body. These are essential fatty acids that the body can't make and must be obtained from what we eat. Linoleic and linolenic play important roles in blood clotting, brain development and inflammation control. Additionally, these essential fatty acids can be converted to other fatty acids that the body needs to function and be healthy.

Fat is our energy bank! It's where we store extra calories that can be used when we do not have access to food. It is also used during exercise when glycogen stores have been depleted.

Fat is also an insulator! It helps us to maintain our body temperature and protects our organs from injury and shock.

Without dietary fat we would not absorb the fat-soluble vitamins A, D, E and K, which all play important roles in health maintenance.

Fat plays a vital role in the brain and nervous system.

It is an important component of cell membranes and plays an important role in skin structure.

And without fat, hormone production would be next to impossible!

Fat also stimulates the flow of bile, emptying of the gallbladder, is a vital component of human milk and is extremely important in infant brain development.

GUIDE TO USING FATS AND OILS

FATS/OILS SAFE FOR FRYING, SAUTÉING AND BROWNING (OPT FOR ORGANIC AND UNREFINED OPTIONS)

Saturated fats are the best options for cooking; since they are chemically stable, they are resistant to damage from heat. Contrary to popular belief, they also play an important role in our health. They provide us with energy, they satiate us and they help us absorb important fat-soluble vitamins such as Vitamins A, D, E and K.

ANIMAL FATS

- Butter
- Ghee
- Lard
- Goose fat
- Duck fat
- Chicken fat (consume in moderation, due to high omega-6 content)
- Tallow (rendered beef or lamb fat)

NON-ANIMAL SATURATED FATS

- Coconut oil
- Palm oil

FATS/OILS SAFE FOR COLD USE

Use in moderation or as a condiment due to high omega-6 content

- Olive oil
- Avocado oil
- Nut oils (macadamia, walnut, etc.)
- Seed oils (sesame, flax, hemp, pumpkin, etc.)

UNHEALTHY FAT/OILS TO AVOID

These fats are either man-made or highly processed. These oils oxidize easily and become rancid, causing inflammation in the body. Avoid anything that is hydrogenated or partially hydrogenated.

- Margarine or other fake butters
- Vegetable oil
- Canola oil
- Corn oil
- Cottonseed oil
- Safflower oil
- Sunflower oil
- Rice bran oil
- Grapeseed oil
- Soybean oil
- Shortening

REFERENCES

The Skinny on Fats by Mary G. Enig, PhD and Sally Fallon // January 1, 2000
"Canola Oil May Be 'Paleo Diet' Approved, But I Won't Eat It" by Diane Sanfilippo // June 14, 2010
"FAQs: What Are Safe Cooking Fats & Oils?" by Diane Sanfilippo // September 19, 2011
"The Definitive Guide to Oils" by Mark Sisson
"A Primal Primer: Animal Fats" by Mark Sisson

TIPS FOR DINING OUT AND TRAVELING

I travel about once a month for work, and here are a few tips that help me keep Paleo on the road.

On the flight: If taking a longer flight, I pack snacks such as nuts, dried fruit, fresh fruit, coconut flakes and beef jerky. Some of these items I might not indulge in often at home, however, they are still much healthier options than snacks served on the plane. I also bring extra snacks for the trip or stop at a store and load up when I arrive, just in case I am in a situation where there isn't something suitable to eat.

You may have to compromise on quality: At home we always use organic and grass-fed ingredients. However, when traveling for work, this is not always an option so I sometimes settle for conventional food as long as it is dairy-, grain-, and legume-free.

Vegetable Oils/Industrial Seed Oils: The major issue with dining out is most foods in restaurants are cooked using vegetable oil (corn oil, soybean oil, cottonseed oil, etc.). I believe this is very unhealthy food, and I try my best to avoid it. I choose dishes that are cooked without oil whenever possible, such as grilled meats and steamed veggies. I have also found it difficult to completely avoid vegetable oil when dining out regularly. In those cases, I focus on staying dairy-, grain-, and legume-free and understand that I may be consuming some vegetable oil. I still try my best to avoid it, but I also try not to worry about it so I can enjoy the meal.

Communication is key: When I first started my current job, I did not mention my Paleo lifestyle to my co-workers, but I always managed to find something to eat regardless of where we went. However, now that they know how I eat, they are accommodating about selecting restaurants and nice about it all. If you explain a little bit about your diet to colleagues, choosing Paleo-friendly restaurants becomes much easier. Maybe you will influence others to make healthier choices, too.

Review restaurant menus in advance: If I know in advance the restaurant where we will be dining, I research the menu and find some options that will work for me before we arrive so it doesn't take me extra time to find that right dish.

Ask the server: If I am unsure about anything, I ask the server questions. They are usually happy to confirm with the chef. I always ask if the fish is farmed or wild caught. I always confirm that the item does not have gluten, because not all ingredients are always listed on the menu. More and more servers are becoming familiar with the term gluten-free. In fact, when I've mentioned that I can't eat gluten, the server has been great about making suggestions.

DINING OUT OPTIONS THAT WORK BEST FOR ME:

American/Continental: These seem to be the easiest places to stay Paleo. I choose foods that are gently cooked or grilled to limit the use of vegetable oils. If I am unsure about any sauces (sometimes flour is added as a thickening agent, or soy sauce, sugar, or vegetable oil are used), I skip the sauce and let the meat and veggies stand on their own.

Salads: The good old go-to! When in doubt, you can always order a salad with meat and ask for olive oil and vinegar for dressing.

Grocery stores with prepared food area (like Whole Foods): You can often get some organic meat and veggies from the prepared meal area. Read the ingredients closely because they sometimes use canola oil.

Mexican food: You can usually get some sort of plate with beef, pork or chicken and ask to substitute the rice and beans for a side of veggies, plus salsa and guacamole.

Thai food: This is always a good option because you can get some sort of vegetable/meat dish or curry and skip the rice. However with most options, you are going to get some vegetable oil. Make sure to choose dishes made without soy sauce. Thai-beef salads are a good option.

Burgers Protein-style: It seems like many places are popping up lately that specialize in grass-fed burgers.

Sushi: I either order sashimi or a hand-roll with no rice, plus some sides. Also, ask if the restaurant has wheat-free soy sauce; most places do now. I personally tolerate white rice pretty well, so every once in a while I might just have rice with my sushi.

WHEN YOUR PARTNER IS NOT PALEO...

In the best-case scenario, the entire family will adopt a Paleo lifestyle. This will definitely help to make it easier to stay committed. However, just because your partner is not committed doesn't mean you can't be. I have been living this way for several years and although my husband mostly eats a Paleo diet, he is not strict. The hardest thing to exclude is the only thing I truly miss—a delicious microbrew! It's difficult to watch my husband enjoy one in the yard on a sunny day. With my intolerance to gluten, cheating here is not an option.

Our deal is all the groceries we buy and meals we cook at home are Paleo-friendly. He cooks paleo meals and agrees that our kids will eat this way. Then he eats what he wants when he or we go out. I will admit when I first started, I wanted badly to "convert" him, I would lecture him over dinner and try to pressure him. I was definitely the "pushy Paleo" wife/sister/daughter/friend. When I eventually got tired and realized my nagging and pleading were not working, I gave up and just tried to lead by example. As he observed my health problems diminish, my energy to become consistent even through my pregnancy, he took it upon himself to decide on a strict 30-day trial.

—ARSY VARTANIAN

FALLING OFF THE PALEO WAGON

It happens to the best of us! To be completely honest, I fell off the Paleo wagon several times prior to making the complete lifestyle change.

In the long run, what has worked for me is the idea that all "cheats" are not created equal. I've found that I react most to gluten. This seems to be true of most people I've talked to. If I momentarily fall of the wagon, I stay focused on avoiding gluten-containing items such as wheat, rye and barley. These foods are the harshest on our bodies. One function of the Paleo diet is to reduce inflammation in the body and improve health and performance by removing food toxins. If you do indulge in a treat such as rice, beans or corn tortilla chips, don't beat yourself up about it, just enjoy it and make sure to get back on track during your next meal.

After a month of eating this way, chances are you won't want to cheat very often. I don't know if there is any scientific evidence on this, but from my own experience and from talking to friends, it seems that after consuming only real foods for a while your tastes change. Sugary foods taste much sweeter than before and artificial foods that you used to love to indulge in (like, in my case, Sour Patch Kids) taste—well, artificial. These foods become less satisfying.

HOW DOES THE PALEO LIFESTYLE REDUCE INFLAMMATION?

Inflammation is caused by an activation of the immune system in response to a stressor. The sources of the stress in our lives are numerous and can be biological (sleep, autoimmune disease, infection), physical (injury, exercise), mental/emotional (work/family/life factors), environmental (chemicals, pollution), and/or dietary (processed foods, unhealthy fats, etc.). While some inflammation is natural, normal and healthy, a prolonged inflammatory state is a catalyst in the development of many diseases. Diabetes, Alzheimer's, cancer, arthritis, heart disease, IBS, Parkinson's and many other conditions are the products of chronic inflammation. Controlling inflammation is crucial in disease prevention and there are generally two ways in which we can accomplish this.

1. Avoid or minimize all agents/conditions that result in an inflammatory response (this is next to impossible).

2. Modify diet and lifestyle to favor an anti-inflammatory state.

HOW DOES A PALEO LIFESTYLE REDUCE INFLAMMATION?

Paleo foods are non-inflammatory foods (for the most part — watch out for high doses of nuts, traditionally raised meats, etc.)

Vegetables are packed with antioxidants and are naturally anti-inflammatory. It is important to eat a variety of vegetables in order to get the most benefit and nutrition.

Many herbs and spices used in paleo cooking have inflammation-reducing properties. Some of the heavy hitters include cumin, basil, capsaicin, garlic, turmeric and oregano.

There are no processed foods which contain unnatural trans fats, refined grains, high doses of sugar, omega-6 fatty acids, and overabundance of chemicals and artificial ingredients.

The paleo eating style emphasizes the importance of limiting the omega-6 fatty acids (inflammatory) and focusing more on the omega-3's (anti-inflammatory). Wild-caught fish and grass-fed meats, minimal amounts of nuts and no processed food are key to achieving an optimal omega-6 to omega-3 ratio.

Paleo promotes a healthy gut! Fermented foods have a place on your plate. Kimchi, sauerkraut, and other fermented vegetables help bolster healthy gut bacteria.

Sensible — not too much, not too little — exercise is promoted. Excessive, high-intensity hammerings drive inflammation. Periodization and a smart training program helps to limit the inflammatory response exercise creates. (Remember, small amounts of inflammation are healthy and natural!)

Good night! Sleep is a key component to a paleo way of life. During sleep is when the body heals and repairs. Lack of sleep results in a natural stress response and therefore results in an inflammatory response.

That's how it works! Paleo is the way to go to reduce and avoid further inflammation. In a world full of stressors it's a great tool!

chapter one

IN THE BEGINNING APPETIZERS

I AM A HUGE FAN OF FINGER FOODS. I love having guests over and serving a variety of appetizers, so guests actually have a chance to mingle. The slow cooker is great for this, as you can prepare the meal in advance and have it warm and ready when guests arrive!

Also guests barely notice they are eating Paleo-friendly foods. So if you serve heavy appetizers as I normally do for a game or party, your guests will have enjoyed a truly Paleo experience. If they weren't drinking beer, you might ask them how they felt the next day. I'll bet they had more energy and felt great.

PALEO **SPICY RIB** APPETIZER

This simple and easy appetizer is great as a finger food and will delight both Paleo and non-Paleo dieting guests.

INGREDIENTS

3 lbs pork spare ribs
2 tbsp paprika
1 tsp chili powder
1 tsp cayenne pepper
1 tsp sweet basil, dried
1 tsp cumin
Salt and pepper just before serving

SAUCE

1 cup tomatoes, peeled and chopped
2 serrano peppers, peeled and chopped
2 tbsp apple cider vinegar
3 cloves garlic, crushed
½ small onion, minced
1 tbsp fresh lime juice
Two pinches of salt

COOKING INSTRUCTIONS

› Cut ribs into single pieces.

› Rub pieces with the spices and place in the slow cooker.

› Put tomatoes in a bowl, smash them with a fork and mix in the rest of the sauce ingredients.

› Pour mixture over the ribs, cover and cook on low for 4-6 hours until ribs are tender.

› Salt and pepper to taste before serving.

SERVINGS: 8

CAPONATA SICILIANA

This dish is usually served chunky, but I often put it through the food processor and make it more of a dip. It makes it much easier when serving with sliced cucumbers. I am a spicy food lover, so I also tend to roast the peppers first and add a couple of jalapeños for some extra kick.

INGREDIENTS

2 bell peppers, chopped
2 large eggplants, peeled and cut into ½-inch pieces
2 tbsp ghee
1 onion, chopped
3-4 cloves garlic, crushed
2 celery stalks, sliced
4 tomatoes, peeled and chopped, cut into ½-inch pieces
2 medium zucchini, cut into ½-inch pieces
2 tbsp apple cider vinegar
¼ cup tomato paste
1 tsp sea salt
¼ tsp ground black pepper
½ cup green or black olives
2 tbsp capers
¼ cup chopped fresh parsley
1 cup chopped fresh basil
¼ cup pine nuts
Salt and pepper to taste
1-2 cucumbers, sliced

COOKING INSTRUCTIONS

› Roast the peppers in the broiler to add some extra flavor, 2-3 minutes a side (an optional step that adds a nice smoky flavor) and transfer to the slow cooker.

› Sauté the eggplants in 1 tablespoon ghee in a heavy-bottomed pan over medium heat until browned on all sides, about 5 minutes, then transfer to the slow cooker.

› Use remaining ghee to sauté the onion, garlic, and celery for 5 minutes, until the onion is translucent, then transfer the mixture to the slow cooker.

› Add the remaining ingredients to the slow cooker except the olives, capers, basil, parsley, pine nuts and cucumbers.

› Cook on low for 4 hours until the vegetables are tender.

› Stir in the olives, capers, parsley, basil and pine nuts.

› Salt and pepper to taste, then serve on cucumber rounds. This dish can be served warm or cold.

SERVINGS: 10-12

HONEY MUSTARD
CAVEMAN DRUMSTICKS

Here's a more traditional and favorite appetizer with a Paleo twist. Honey is Paleo-friendly but not encouraged in large amounts. Here it is a bit of a treat. The longer you stay on the Paleo diet, the more sensitive you will become to sweet flavors and the less you will desire to sweeten things.

INGREDIENTS

3 lbs chicken drumsticks

Salt and pepper for browning and just before serving

¼ cup coconut oil

⅓ cup honey

2 tbsp stone-ground mustard

3 cloves garlic, crushed

COOKING INSTRUCTIONS

- Salt and pepper drumsticks and brown them in a broiler for 5 minutes, turning once.
- Each broiler is different so watch closely to make sure drumsticks don't burn.
- Meanwhile, melt the coconut oil and mix it with the rest of the ingredients in a large bowl.
- Place browned chicken in bowl and mix until coated with the sauce.
- Pour everything into the slow cooker and cook on low heat for 5 hours.
- Salt and pepper the drumsticks before serving.

SERVINGS: 8

LAMB **MEATBALLS**

Grass-fed lamb is a great way to get more nutritents into your diet. This dish has a Middle-Eastern flair with the cumin and is a favorite among my friends, even those who don't usually eat lamb.

INGREDIENTS

1 tbsp ghee
2 lbs ground lamb
2 tsp cumin
2 tsp fennel
1 tsp cayenne pepper
½ tsp turmeric
Pinch of saffron
2 large eggs, lightly beaten
¼ white onion, finely minced
3 cloves garlic, crushed
¼ cup beef or chicken stock
Salt and pepper just before serving
Toothpicks for serving

COOKING INSTRUCTIONS

- Heat ghee in a frying pan over medium heat.
- Mix all remaining ingredients, except the stock, in a bowl to combine well.
- Shape into meatballs and drop into the pan.
- Brown for 5 minutes, turning the meatballs once.
- Add meatballs to the slow cooker.
- Add stock, cover and cook on low for 3-4 hours.

SERVINGS: 6

CILANTRO MINT PESTO SAUCE (OPTIONAL)

INGREDIENTS

3 tbsp olive oil
1 tbsp lemon juice
1 tsp fresh ginger
2 cups cilantro
1 cup mint
½ cup chopped onion
2 cloves garlic, crushed
salt and pepper
½ jalapeño pepper, chopped

COOKING INSTRUCTIONS

To make the sauce, place all ingredients in a food processor and mix until smooth.

CURRIED **CHICKEN WINGS**

Here's a different take on chicken wings that I love. They are really easy to make so I whip them up when we have last-minute guests over to watch a game, and the wings are often gone before game time.

INGREDIENTS

4 lbs chicken wings
1 cup coconut milk
2 tbsp fish sauce
3 tbsp red curry paste
¼ cup onion, minced
2 cloves garlic, crushed
2 tsp grated fresh ginger
Salt and pepper before serving

COOKING INSTRUCTIONS

- Broil the chicken wings for 5 minutes, turning once, watching carefully so they don't burn.
- Mix all remaining ingredients, then place sauce and chicken in the slow cooker and cook on low for 4-5 hours.
- Remove the chicken to a serving dish, and thicken the sauce by cooking it on the stovetop over medium-high heat, stirring constantly, for 1-2 minutes.
- Pour the sauce over the wings, salt and pepper to taste and serve.

SERVINGS: 10-12

CONDIMENTS & SUBSTITUTIONS

Condiments tend to be a matter of personal preference in the Paleo lifestyle. Depending on your goals or health concerns you may be stricter or less strict than me.

Here is my approach: I'm comfortable using non-paleo condiments in my cooking, as long as they are in small amounts, and I don't have an adverse reaction to them. What I mean by non-paleo is that they may have sugar or soy in them. However, I never use condiments that have wheat in them.

THE MAIN CONDIMENTS THAT YOU MAY NOTICE ME USING ARE:

Tamari (gluten-free soy sauce): Which is actually just fermented soybeans, but I say gluten-free because the first ingredient in conventional soy sauce is wheat and not soy so make sure to read the label. If you choose not to use any soy in your diet, you can always substitute coconut aminos. Coconut aminos have a similar salty flavor with a slight sweetness.

Another ingredient I will occasionally use with Asian dishes is **mirin**, which is rice wine vinegar. If you choose to not include any rice products in your diet, you can always substitute coconut vinegar for mirin.

From time to time, I will use **Worcestershire sauce**. Again, make sure to read the label to ensure that there is no wheat in it. If you choose not to include non-paleo condiments, you can always skip this ingredient.

Cooking with alcohol: You will notice that several recipes use fruit-based alcohol like wine, brandy, cognac or hard cider. Most of the alcohol used in these recipes evaporates as it cooks. However if you're sensitive to alcohol or don't want to use it, here are a few alternatives for ensuring that the meat stays tender: broth, apple juice, tomato juice or blanched tomatoes and filtered water.

Ghee and grass-fed butter: Although not strictly paleo, these are still a healthy fat choice. Butter is a good source of vitamin K-2, which has been found to help protect us from heart disease. It promotes brain function and even helps prevent cancer. Once the milk is removed, butter is left with very minimal traces of lactose and casein (the main problems with dairy) and ghee is left with even less. I also prefer these fats for browning, as they don't compromise the flavor of the dish with other strong flavors like bacon when using bacon grease. If you are sensitive to butter and ghee, or you choose not to use them, refer to my guide for using fats and oils on page 14. I almost always brown my meats and veggies using ghee, but if ghee is hard to find in your area, butter will always do!

Cooking liquids: We prefer to make our own cooking liquids (see page 234) as it is easy and much healthier. When testing my recipes, I always used homemade coconut milk, broth and blanched tomatoes. However, if there are time constraints, canned varieties can also be substituted.

Tomato paste: Tomato paste is a great ingredient for adding flavor to slow-cooker meals. I highly urge you to find a variety sold in a glass jar, opposed to in a can.

AUTOIMMUNE DISORDERS

The prevalence of autoimmune disease in today's society seems to be skyrocketing. The diseases are many: celiac, diabetes, rheumatoid arthritis, lupus, thyroid maladies, MS, ALS, fibromyalgia, Crohn's, ulcerative colitis, etc. Autoimmune disorders refer to any and all conditions in which the body cannot distinguish between foreign materials/ proteins and itself. Then the body begins attacking its own tissues and organs. It is believed that 70% of autoimmune disease can be blamed on environmental or lifestyle elements. Some believe that "leaky gut" or increased intestinal permeability is a key factor in the development of autoimmune conditions. Many dietary components contribute to the development of leaky gut. Some of the most common offenders are wheat, grains, legumes, dairy and nightshade vegetables; NSAIDS, oral contraceptives and antacids can also play roles in leaky-gut development. Avoiding the foods and agents that contribute to the development and progression of autoimmune conditions can remarkably improve health which is one of the reasons the Paleo lifestyle has become so popular.

Those with pre-existing autoimmune conditions are advised to follow an "Autoimmune Paleo" protocol. In this plan nightshade vegetables (peppers, potatoes, eggplant, green tomatoes, and other capsaicin-containing veggies), eggs and nuts are also excluded due to possible reactions. These guidelines may be loosened in time based on individual response and progression.

chapter two

SAVORY, SUCCULENT AND SLOW-COOKED **BEEF DISHES**

BEEF AND RED MEAT IN GENERAL HAVE RECEIVED MUCH MISGUIDED NEGATIVE ATTENTION IN THE MAINSTREAM. We now believe that choosing healthy beef from grass-fed cattle has proven health benefits. Beef is not only an excellent source of protein, but also of B vitamins, iron and zinc! Studies have found that grass-fed beef is higher in Omega-3 fatty acids, conjugated linoleic acid (CLA) and vitamin E! Omega-3s are present in the grass eaten by cattle; when cows eat grain they don't store this essentially fatty acid to pass on to us. By choosing grass-fed beef we are also avoiding digesting hormones, antibiotics and other drugs. Grass feeding is also better for the animals and the environment. It promotes humane treatment of animals and reduces the use of chemical fertilizers and pesticides to grow unsustainable amounts of corn and soy.

When making a health-conscious choice about eating animal proteins, we shouldn't ask ourselves, is this red or white meat? We should ask, did this animal eat what it was naturally meant to eat?

Grass-fed beef can be pricey. Purchasing through a CSA is a great way to save money. Also, purchasing tough, inexpensive cuts such as roasts and cooking them gently and slowly in a slow cooker is another great way to incorporate grass-fed meat into our diets.

TRADITIONAL **BEEF BOURGUIGNON**

This French twist on a regular beef stew conatins less sauce, is more elegant and delivers a delicious tangy red-wine flavor that is to die for. Shallots can be time consuming to peel so feel free to save shallots for guests and swap in a large yellow onion cut into eighths for regular meals, though I'm not sure who would call this a "regular meal." It's easy gourmet French country cooking at its best and will fill your house with tantalizing aromas all day, presaging the great meal ahead.

INGREDIENTS

½ lb bacon, diced
2 lbs beef chuck, cut into big cubes
8 shallots, peeled and left whole
2 cloves garlic, crushed
1 tbsp Herbes de Provence
1 lb mushrooms, stems removed and sliced
1 lb carrots, sliced
1½ cups red wine
1 cup beef stock
½ cup cognac
Salt and pepper just before serving

COOKING INSTRUCTIONS

- Sauté the bacon over medium high until just crisp, about 3-5 minutes.
- Remove the bacon and brown the meat in the bacon grease in batches for about 5 minutes each, turning the meat only a few times and allowing it to brown well.
- If the bacon grease is smoking, turn the heat down to medium.
- Place the beef, bacon and all other ingredients into the slow cooker and cook on low for 6-8 hours.
- You may have extra liquid, so use a slotted spoon to serve the meat and vegetables in a bowl and then ladle just enough sauce over the dish to cover the bottom of the bowl.
- Season liberally with salt and pepper before serving.

SERVINGS: 6

COOK'S NOTE: SLOW COOKING DRAWS THE SALT OUT OF MEATS AND VEGETABLES SO IT'S BEST TO ADD A GOOD AMOUNT OF SALT JUST BEFORE SERVING TO BRING OUT THE FLAVORS.

BEEF AND FENNEL STEW

The fennel gives this dish Mediterranean flair and a lighter flavor. I'd recommend you brown the beef for this one to give the dish more body. As with almost all beef stews, the homemade bone broth offers big health benefits and is packed with minerals that are great for your body.

INGREDIENTS

2 lbs beef stew meat
1 onion, chopped
1 tbsp ghee
2 fennel bulbs, cored and thinly sliced
2 carrots, cored and sliced
1 bell pepper, chopped
2 cloves garlic, smashed
3 cups beef broth
2 tbsp tomato paste
1 tsp fennel seeds
1 tsp paprika
1 tsp thyme
2 bay leaves
Salt and pepper just before serving

COOKING INSTRUCTIONS

› Brown the meat in batches in a heavy-bottomed pan over medium-high heat for 5 minutes.

› Be careful not to crowd the pan and make sure it is well heated before you put in the meat.

› Sauté onion in the ghee until translucent.

› Put all the other ingredients in the slow cooker with the meat and cook on low for 8 hours.

› Salt and pepper to taste before serving.

SERVINGS: 6

OXTAIL SOUP

This is a very nutrient-dense meal, rich in gelatin which builds strong bones and is good for your skin, heart and muscles. This rich dish is also very tasty, sort of a supercharged beef stew. When following the Paleo diet, fatty and nutrient-rich meals stop you from overeating while keeping you satisfied naturally by providing what your body needs. You don't need to starve yourself to stay fit.

INGREDIENTS

3 lbs oxtails, cut into sections
1 onion, chopped
2 large carrots, sliced
1 large leek, cleaned well and sliced
2 bay leaves
1 red spicy pepper (optional)
3 cups beef stock
1 cup red wine
2 tomatoes, peeled and chopped
1 tsp thyme
¼ cup chopped parsley
Salt and pepper just before serving

COOKING INSTRUCTIONS

› Brown the oxtail in batches in a heavy-bottomed pan over medium-high heat for about 5 minutes each batch, then transfer to the slow cooker.

› Put all ingredients into the slow cooker except the parsley.

› Cook for 8 hours on low heat.

› Stir in parsley, then add salt and pepper before serving.

SERVINGS: 6-8

BEEF BRISKET IN ESPRESSO BEAN BBQ SAUCE

This is a great recipe for hosting an outdoor party in the summer. You can prepare it in advance and keep it warm in the pot on your counter or plugged in outside. This dish is nicely balanced, not too sweet or sugary like some barbecue sauces but full of flavor. Brisket is a lean cut of meat so is a good option for people restricting calories and works well for the crockpot, a tough cut that comes out nice and fork-tender. This dish takes a little extra prep time but is worth it.

INGREDIENTS

ESPRESSO BBQ SAUCE

1 medium onion, diced
2 tbsp ghee
4 cloves garlic, crushed
2 dried chipotle peppers
5 whole tomatoes, peeled and seeds removed
½ cup apple cider vinegar
Juice of 1 lemon
½ cup honey
1 tsp smoked paprika
¼ tsp grated fresh ginger
¼ cup brewed espresso or ½ cup strong regular coffee
2 tbsp Dijon mustard
2 tbsp gluten-free Worcestershire sauce
2 tsp chili powder
½ tbsp salt
½ tbsp pepper

2½ lbs beef brisket
Salt and pepper just before serving

COOKING INSTRUCTIONS

- To make the sauce, sauté the onion with ghee in a large saucepan over medium heat until translucent, about 8 minutes.
- Add garlic and chipotle peppers, and sauté until the garlic is fragrant, about 3 minutes. Add tomatoes and simmer for a few minutes.
- Using either an immersion blender or food processor, puree the mixture.
- Return the pan to medium heat, put the pureed barbecue sauce in the pan and add the rest of the sauce ingredients.
- Stir everything together until completely combined and continue to cook at a low simmer for about 30 minutes, stirring occasionally, until the sauce is thickened and a dark burgundy color.
- Brown the brisket in a clean pan over medium-high heat for 5 minutes.
- Place in the slow cooker with 1 cup of the barbecue sauce.
- Save second cup to serve directly on the meat.
- Cook on low for 6-8 hours, then shred the brisket in the slow cooker with 2 forks, being careful not to burn your hands on the sides.
- Salt and pepper before serving.

SERVINGS: 6

ROPA VIEJA

The slow cooker is a great way to cook this traditional Latin American dish. While it is traditionally served with rice, I like it over steamed vegetables.

INGREDIENTS

2 tbsp ghee
2 onions, sliced
2 bell peppers, sliced (1 red and 1 green to add some color)
4 cloves garlic, minced
2½ lbs chuck roast
8 tomatoes, peeled, seeded and chopped
2 tbsp tomato paste
½ cup beef broth
1 tbsp cumin
1 tsp oregano
1 tsp smoked paprika
1 tsp salt
½ tsp pepper
Fresh cilantro for garnish
Salt and pepper just before serving

COOKING INSTRUCTIONS

› Melt ghee in a heavy-bottomed pan over medium heat and sauté the onions until translucent.

› Add the peppers and garlic, sauté another 3 minutes, until garlic is fragrant, then transfer to the slow cooker.

› Brown the roast on all sides in the same pan over medium-high heat for about 5 minutes, then transfer to the slow cooker.

› Stir together tomatoes, tomato paste, broth, spices, salt and pepper in a large bowl. Pour over the beef and cook on low for 6-7 hours.

› Shred the beef in the slow cooker with 2 forks, and cook for an additional hour.

SERVINGS: 4-6

COOK'S NOTE: WHEN THE BEEF IS READY, IT SHOULD SHRED EASILY. IF YOU END UP WITH TOO MUCH LIQUID, TASTE THE MEAT, AND IF YOU ARE HAPPY WITH THE FLAVORS JUST REMOVE THE MEAT AND VEGETABLES WITH A SLOTTED SPOON. IF IT NEEDS MORE FLAVOR, YOU CAN MOVE THE DISH TO A SAUTÉ PAN AND SIMMER ON LOW FOR 30 MINUTES TO CONCENTRATE THE FLAVORS AND REDUCE THE LIQUID.

CHILI COLORADO

This dish is easy to make and a good alternative to a typical comfort food meal at the end of a long day. It features bold Southwestern flavors that are classic favorites.

INGREDIENTS

1 onion, chopped
1 tbsp butter
3 lbs stew beef, cut into 1-inch chunks
8 dried chiles, stems and seeds removed
2 tbsp tomato paste
3 cloves garlic, chopped
2 cups beef stock
1 tbsp chili powder
2 tsp cumin
1 tbsp dried oregano
1 tsp dried parsley
4 tomatoes, peeled and chopped
Fresh chopped cilantro for garnish
Salt and pepper just before serving

COOKING INSTRUCTIONS

› Lightly sauté onion in the butter in a heavy-bottomed pan over medium heat, about 8 minutes or until the onion is translucent.

› Add to the slow cooker.

› Return the pan to the heat, increased to medium high.

› Brown the beef on all sides in batches for 5 minutes a batch.

› Add the browned beef and all other ingredients to the slow cooker and cook on low for 8 hours.

› Salt and pepper to taste before serving.

SERVINGS: 6

SHORT RIBS
IN TOMATO FENNEL SAUCE

This is one of the easiest recipes I know. The light flavor of fennel pairs nicely with the rich tomato sauce to create a terrific, fork-tender dish for a summer evening while barely lifting a finger.

INGREDIENTS

8 short ribs
4 cloves garlic, crushed
1 onion, diced
2 carrots, sliced
1 fennel bulb, chopped
6 tomatoes, peeled and chopped or 1 (14-oz) can of whole tomatoes
1 tsp paprika
1 cup beef broth
½ cup red wine
1 red chili pepper
½ tsp thyme
½ tsp oregano
2 bay leaves
Salt and pepper just before serving

COOKING INSTRUCTIONS

› Put all the ingredients into the slow cooker and cook on low for 4-6 hours.

› Be careful not to overcook or the meat will slide off the bones before you get them out of the slow cooker.

› Salt and pepper to taste, then serve.

SERVINGS: 2-3

PALEO **BEEF CASSEROLE**

This is a great inexpensive one-dish meal. It's very satisfying and the perfect meal right after a workout. It has carbs, fat and protein! Protein is extremely important to muscle recovery, growth and regeneration.

INGREDIENTS

1 onion, diced
1 tbsp ghee
3-4 cloves garlic
2 lbs ground beef
1 tsp dried oregano
1 tsp dried basil
3 yams, peeled and thinly sliced
1 green pepper, seeded and chopped
1 red bell pepper, seeded and chopped
1 cup sliced mushrooms
1 cup tomato sauce
Salt and pepper just before serving

COOKING INSTRUCTIONS

› In a large frying pan set over medium heat, sauté the onion in ghee for 5 minutes. Add the garlic and cook until fragrant, about 3 minutes.

› Turn the heat to medium high and add the ground beef, breaking up the meat with a spatula.

› Add the oregano and basil to the meat as it is browning.

› Cook for another 5 minutes.

› Lay the yams on the bottom of the slow cooker, then add the green and red peppers and mushrooms.

› Place the beef on top and pour tomato sauce over it.

› Cook on low for 6 hours.

SERVINGS: 6

PRIME RIB CHILI

This is an upscale chili with a more sophisticated and gourmet taste. There's no chili powder; the fresh peppers do the work here and deliver a nice, more subtle flavor. Beans are not Paleo-friendly so are not included but you won't miss them.

INGREDIENTS

3 lbs beef prime rib, cubed
2 tbsp ghee
1 white onion, diced
3 cloves garlic, crushed
2 Anaheim peppers, seeded and diced
1 poblano pepper, seeded and diced
1 serrano pepper, seeded and diced
1 red bell pepper, chopped
6 tomatoes, peeled and chopped
2 tbsp tomato paste
2 cups beef stock
2 tsp smoked paprika
¼ tsp cayenne pepper
1 tsp cumin
1 tsp oregano
Salt and pepper just before serving
¼ cup chopped fresh cilantro, for garnish

COOKING INSTRUCTIONS

› Brown the beef in 1 tablespoon of ghee in a heavy-bottomed pan over medium-high heat for 5 minutes and place in the slow cooker.

› Lower the temperature to medium and sauté the onion, garlic and peppers in the remaining ghee for 5 minutes, until the onion is translucent.

› Place vegetables in the slow cooker with the remaining ingredients and spices.

› Be sure to stir in the tomato paste so it is well incorporated.

› Cook on low for 6-8 hours.

SERVINGS: 6-8

COOK'S NOTE: YOU CAN ADD A NICE SMOKY FLAVOR BY BROILING THE PEPPERS FOR 5 MINUTES BEFORE CHOP-PING THEM.

BEEF ROAST WITH CHILES

This is a nice twist on a traditional pot roast, giving it a Tex-Mex flavor.

INGREDIENTS

3-4 lbs beef brisket
1 tsp cumin
1 tsp caraway seeds
1 tsp ground fennel seeds
1 large onion, chopped
2 tbsp ghee
2 cloves garlic, crushed
6 dried chiles, chopped, plus more whole chiles for garnish (optional)
1 cup beef broth
Salt and pepper just before serving

COOKING INSTRUCTIONS

› Rub beef with spices, except the chiles.

› Sauté onion in 1 tablespoon of ghee in a heavy-bottomed pan over medium heat, about 5 minutes.

› Place in the slow cooker.

› Turn heat to medium high and brown the beef on all sides in the remaining tablespoon of ghee, about 6 minutes.

› Add the rest of the ingredients to the slow cooker and cook on low for 8 hours.

› Salt and pepper to taste and serve. If serving to guests, garnish platter with additional whole chiles.

SERVINGS: 6-8

BEEF **BRISKET**

A classic dish that's naturally Paleo-friendly, brisket offers easy flavors for the whole family. It freezes well and makes perfect leftovers for great Paleo lunches and fast dinners. I highly recommend you make your own broth for these and other dishes. You'll taste a big difference in the flavor, and the homemade broth has a greater nutritional value than bouillon cubes or canned stock.

INGREDIENTS

3-4 lbs beef brisket
3-4 shallots, peeled
2 parsnips, chopped (you can substitute 2 carrots)
2 tomatoes, peeled and chopped
2 bay leaves
1 cup beef broth
2 tbsp apple cider vinegar
2 tbsp chili powder
1 tsp dry mustard
Salt and pepper just before serving

COOKING INSTRUCTIONS

› Preheat a heavy-bottomed pan to medium high for a couple minutes and brown the brisket on all sides for about 6-8 minutes.

› Transfer the meat to the slow cooker.

› Add the rest of the ingredients to the slow cooker, making sure the dried spices are mixed into the liquid and not clumped or sitting dry on top of the meat.

› Cook on low for 6-8 hours.

› Add a good amount of salt and pepper, slice against the grain and serve in slices, spooning the sauce over the meat.

SERVINGS: 8-10

THAI **RED BEEF CURRY**

I love Thai food. I usually eat it with a side of steamed vegetables instead of rice. The lemongrass in this dish makes the flavor nice and light.

INGREDIENTS

2 lbs beef, cut into slices ⅛- to ¼-inch thick
2 tbsp coconut oil
2 cups of coconut milk
3 tbsp Thai red curry paste
3 kaffir lime leaves
2 small Asian eggplants, sliced
2 tbsp chopped peeled fresh ginger
3 cloves garlic, crushed
1 stalk lemongrass, finely sliced
1 tsp coriander
1 tsp cumin
2 tsp chili powder
Salt and pepper just before serving

COOKING INSTRUCTIONS

› Brown the beef in coconut oil in a heavy-bottomed pan over medium-high heat for 6 minutes.

› Place meat in slow cooker.

› Add the rest of the ingredients.

› Cook on low for 6-8 hours.

› Salt and pepper to taste, then serve.

SERVINGS: 4-6

LEMONGRASS AND CASHEW **BEEF**

Lemongrass in this dish is strong and underscored by the lime leaves. The cashews add a nice surprising crunch for a full-flavored Asian meal.

INGREDIENTS

2 tbsp fish sauce
1 tbsp honey
2 tbsp minced shallots
3 cloves garlic, crushed
1 tsp cayenne pepper
½ tbsp powdered coriander
2 stalks lemongrass, thinly sliced
3-4 kaffir lime leaves
1 tbsp grated fresh ginger
½ cup coconut aminos
2 lbs flank steak, thickly sliced
1 onion, cut into wedges
2 red bell peppers, sliced
¼ cup coarsely crushed cashews
4 scallions, cut into ½-inch lengths
Salt and pepper just before serving

COOKING INSTRUCTIONS

› Put the fish sauce, honey, shallots, garlic, cayenne pepper, coriander, lemongrass, lime leaves, ginger and coconut aminos into the slow cooker.

› Stir until combined.

› Place the beef, onion and bell peppers into the slow cooker with the sauce.

› Cook on low for 4-6 hours.

› Add cashews and half the scallions 30 minutes before serving.

› Garnish with the remaining scallions. Salt and pepper to taste, then serve.

SERVINGS: 4-6

PERSIAN STEW WITH OKRA (BAAMIEH)

Okra is a seasonal vegetable that is not always easy to find. Every time I spot it, I snatch some up to make this traditional Persian stew. This dish is usually served over basmati rice so try it over cauliflower rice.

INGREDIENTS

2 tbsp ghee
1 large onion, diced
2 lbs beef chuck, cut into 1-inch pieces
4 cloves garlic, crushed
½ tsp turmeric
4 fresh tomatoes, peeled and chopped
2 tbsp tomato paste
½ cup beef broth
1 lb okra, stems cut off
2 tbsp fresh lime juice
Salt and pepper just before serving

COOKING INSTRUCTIONS

› Melt 2 tablespoons ghee in a heavy-bottomed pan over medium-high heat and sauté the onion until soft, about 5 minutes.

› Add the meat, garlic and ¼ teaspoon of the turmeric.

› Sauté until meat is browned, about another 6 minutes, being careful not to burn the garlic.

› Add tomatoes and tomato paste and sauté for 3 minutes longer.

› Transfer meat mixture from the pan to the slow cooker.

› Add the broth and cook on low for 6 hours.

› Add okra and cook for an additional 1 hour. Make sure not to overcook the okra, which can become slimy.

› Add the remaining ¼ teaspoon turmeric and the lime juice, then salt and pepper to taste before serving.

SERVINGS: 6

COOK'S NOTE: TRIM THE STEMS OF THE OKRA, BUT MAKE SURE NOT TO REMOVE ANY OF THE BASE.

SPICY THAI **BEEF SOUP**

I just love Thai food. It offers interesting flavors, and is sweet and savory. A childhood friend was Thai, so I grew up eating Thai food with her family. This is a tangy and satisfying soup with nice flavors of kaffir and lemongrass. Be warned that Thai restaurants use a lot of soy sauce, so it's better to make it at home so you can keep it Paleo-friendly.

INGREDIENTS

4 cups beef stock
2 stalks lemongrass, cut into pieces
4-5 kaffir lime leaves
4 red chili peppers
4 cloves garlic, crushed
1 lb thinly sliced beef
2-3 tbsp lime juice
2 tbsp fish sauce
2 tbsp red curry paste
¼ tsp cayenne pepper
Salt and pepper just before serving
2 scallions, chopped, for garnish

COOKING INSTRUCTIONS

› Put all the ingredients into the slow cooker.

› Cook on low for 4-6 hours until meat is tender.

› Salt and pepper to taste, and garnish with chopped scallions just before serving.

SERVINGS: 6

BEEF AND **BOK CHOY**

These ingredients are a popular combination in Asian cooking. The subtle flavors balance nicely in this light sauce with ginger adding a fresh zest. P.S. Don't use sesame oil to brown the meat. Use butter, ghee or coconut oil.

INGREDIENTS

2 lbs flank steak, cut lengthwise into 1-inch-thick strips
1 tbsp ghee
1 onion, sliced
4 cloves garlic, crushed
2 tbsp fresh minced ginger
½ cup beef broth
2 tbsp sesame oil
¼ cup coconut aminos or Tamari
5 cups bok choy, trimmed and cut into 1-inch pieces
1 red chili pepper, seeded and sliced
Salt and pepper just before serving
Green onions for garnish

COOKING INSTRUCTIONS

› In a heavy-bottomed pan over medium heat, sear the beef on all sides for about 5 minutes and place in the slow cooker.

› Add the ghee to the pan and sauté onion for 5 minutes, until translucent.

› Add the garlic and cook another 3 minutes, until fragrant.

› Place onion and remaining ingredients in the slow cooker.

› Cook on low for 6-8 hours.

› Salt and pepper to taste and garnish with green onions.

SERVINGS: 4-6

PICADILLO

The slow cooker does really well with ground meats, which are also a great affordable way to eat grass-fed meat. This dish transforms regular old ground beef into a Cuban delight, with the surprising taste of olives adding an exotic and well-balanced flavor. It is also as a nice complement to eggs for breakfast.

INGREDIENTS

2 small onions, chopped
2 tbsp ghee
4 cloves garlic, crushed
3 lbs ground beef
½ cup beef stock
4 tomatoes, chopped
2 tbsp tomato paste
1 jalapeño pepper, finely chopped
1 bell pepper, chopped
1 tsp dried oregano
1 tsp dried basil
1 tsp cumin
½ lb pitted green olives
Salt and pepper just before serving

COOKING INSTRUCTIONS

› Sauté onions in ghee in a heavy-bottomed pan over medium-high heat for 5 minutes, or until translucent.

› Add the garlic and brown the meat for 5 minutes, stirring occasionally to make sure the onions and garlic don't burn.

› Place meat, garlic and onions in the slow cooker with all remaining ingredients, except the olives.

› Cook on low for 6-8 hours.

› Add olives in the last hour of cooking.

› Salt and pepper to taste, then serve.

SERVINGS: 6-8

INDIAN **BEEF CURRY**

This very flavorful dish has a lot of health benefits. Turmeric is a spice with anti-inflamatory properties. It is thought that cinnamon helps lower blood-sugar levels and increases insulin production in the body, but I eat it because I love the exotic flavors.

INGREDIENTS

3 tbsp ghee
2 lbs beef roast, cubed
1 onion, sliced
2 cloves garlic, crushed
1 tbsp grated fresh ginger
1 tbsp ground coriander
2 tsp cumin
4 dried red chiles
1 tsp turmeric
1 tsp cinnamon
1 cup coconut milk
½ cup beef broth
Juice of 1 lemon
Salt and pepper just before serving

COOKING INSTRUCTIONS

› Heat a heavy-bottomed pan over medium high.

› Melt 1 tablespoon of ghee and then brown the beef in 2 or 3 batches, about 5 minutes each batch.

› Lower the heat to medium and sauté the onion and garlic in the remaining ghee for 5 minutes, until translucent.

› Transfer to the slow cooker.

› Add the rest of the ingredients to the slow cooker.

› Cook on low for 6-8 hours.

› Salt and pepper to taste, then serve.

SERVINGS: 4-6

BEEF KALDERETA

Liver is a Paleo superfood, as I might have mentioned before. Many people are not huge fans of liver, or not familiar with the taste. This may be the perfect dish to help you include liver in your diet, as it hides the strong flavor a bit.

INGREDIENTS

2 lbs chuck roast, cut into chunks
2 tbsp butter
3 onions, chopped
3 bell peppers, diced
6 cloves garlic, crushed
½ lb chicken liver
6 tomatoes, finely chopped
1 cup tomato sauce
2 cups beef stock
3 hot chili peppers, chopped
3 yams, cut into chunks
2 bay leaves
Salt and pepper just before serving

COOKING INSTRUCTIONS

- In a heavy-bottomed pan, brown the beef in 1 tablespoon of butter in batches over medium heat, about 5 minutes a batch.
- Transfer to the slow cooker.
- Sauté the onions and bell peppers in the remaining butter until onions are translucent, about 5 minutes. Add the garlic and sauté until fragrant, about 3 minutes.
- Meanwhile, chop the liver by pulsing it in a food processor.
- Add all the ingredients into the slow cooker.
- Cook on low for 6-8 hours.
- Salt and pepper to taste, then serve.

SERVINGS: 4-6

CROCKPOT KOREAN BEEF (BULGOGI)

This recipe has a nice tangy twist. It goes really well with kimchi. Don't forget to allow time to marinate the meat.

INGREDIENTS

4 cloves garlic, crushed
2 tbsp coconut vinegar or mirin
4 tbsp coconut aminos or Tamari
2 tbsp sesame oil
1 tbsp honey
2 lbs flank steak, thinly sliced
½ onion, chopped
1 tbsp ghee
Salt and pepper just before serving

COOKING INSTRUCTIONS

- Mix all the ingredients except meat, onion and ghee in a bowl.
- Pour marinade over meat and marinate for at least a few hours or up to overnight in the refrigerator.
- Remove meat from marinade and let stand to dry a bit.
- Reserve the marinade.
- Sauté the onion in the ghee in a heavy-bottomed pan over medium heat for 5 minutes, until translucent.
- Transfer to the slow cooker.
- Turn the heat up to medium high and brown the meat in batches for about 5 minutes each batch.
- Place in slow cooker.
- Add the marinade to the slow cooker.
- Cook on low for 6-8 hours.

SERVINGS: 4-6

CABBAGE **DOLMAS**

This is a more involved recipe, but worth it. It's my mom's recipe and was a childhood favorite of mine. She cooked it on the stove top with rice, but I adapted it for the slow cooker and made it Paleo friendly. It has a lot of flavor and is very filling and satisfying. I usually make a large amount and freeze some for later use.

INGREDIENTS

1 large onion, finely chopped
3 ripe tomatoes, 1 finely chopped and 2 peeled and coarsely chopped
2 tbsp tomato paste
3 cloves garlic, crushed
½ cup finely minced fresh mint leaves
1 cup finely minced fresh parsley
¼ tsp cayenne pepper
1 tbsp cumin
2 tsp salt
1 tsp pepper
½ cup olive oil, plus more for drizzling
2 lbs ground beef
20 white cabbage leaves
Salt and pepper just before serving

COOKING INSTRUCTIONS

› To make the stuffing, combine the onion, finely chopped tomato, tomato paste, garlic, herbs, spices, salt, pepper, olive oil and beef.

› If necessary, cut down the cabbage leaves so they aren't too big for a tablespoon of the stuffing.

› Blanch the cabbage leaves by dunking them in boiling water for 1 minute.

› Place 1 heaping tablespoon of stuffing in the middle of each cabbage leaf.

› Make into dolmas by folding the top and bottom over the filling, and then folding in the sides and rolling like a small burrito.

› Arrange dolmas in the slow cooker.

› Add the remaining tomatoes, then drizzle with olive oil.

› Put a heatproof plate that fits in the slow cooker on top of dolmas, to weigh them down and keep leaves from opening.

› Cook on low for 4-6 hours.

› Salt and pepper to taste, then serve.

SERVINGS: 4-6

COOK'S NOTE: TO REHEAT A FROZEN DOLMA, PUT IT IN A PAN IN THE OVEN OR PLACE IT IN A TOASTER OVEN ON 350 DEGREES FOR 15 MINUTES.

STUFFED **EGGPLANT**

This is a fun dish to serve and comes with its own vegetable bowls. Here the mint lightens up the rich flavor of the ground beef. Armenians put a lot of mint in their food, but we aren't sure if this is a traditional dish or not. It's just tasty.

INGREDIENTS

6 eggplants
1 lb ground beef
1 tbsp chopped fresh basil
2 tbsp chopped fresh mint leaves
1 tsp cumin
⅛ tsp cayenne pepper
Salt and pepper to taste, plus more for serving
2 cloves garlic, minced
2 tbsp ghee
½ red onion, minced
2 Anaheim peppers, diced
3 tomatoes, peeled and chopped

COOKING INSTRUCTIONS

› Cut eggplants lengthwise and scoop out the inside and reserve, leaving the shell about ½ inch thick.

› Cube the eggplant meat.

› Mix the ground beef with basil, mint, cumin, cayenne, salt, pepper and garlic.

› Heat the ghee in a heavy-bottomed pan over medium high and sauté the onion, peppers, approximately one-third of the tomatoes and all the cubed eggplant for 5 minutes, or until the onions are translucent.

› Add the ground beef and brown for 6 minutes, breaking up the meat with a wooden spoon or spatula.

› Scoop the mixture into the eggplant shells and place them in the slow cooker.

› Arrange the rest of the tomatoes around the eggplants.

› Cook on low for 3-4 hours.

› Salt and pepper to taste, then serve.

SERVINGS: 6

STUFFED **PEPPERS**

This traditional dish is great in the slow cooker if you are careful when removing the perfectly done peppers. Each one is a hearty and delicious meal nicely presented.

INGREDIENTS

6 large peppers
2 lbs ground beef
½ cup finely chopped flat-leaf parsley
¼ cup finely chopped fresh basil
1 tbsp dried oregano
1 tbsp cumin
1 tsp salt
½ tsp pepper
1 onion, minced
3 cloves garlic, crushed
3 tomatoes, peeled and chopped
½ cup beef broth
Salt and pepper just before serving

COOKING INSTRUCTIONS

› Wash peppers, cut off the stems and clean the insides.

› Mix ground beef with herbs, cumin, salt, pepper, onion, and garlic.

› Lightly brown the mixture in a heavy-bottomed pan over medium heat for 5 minutes, breaking up the beef.

› Stuff the peppers with the mixture and arrange in the slow cooker.

› Place tomatoes around the peppers and pour in the broth.

› Cook on low for 4-6 hours.

› Salt and pepper to taste, then serve.

SERVINGS: 6

VENISON THYME STEW
WITH YAMS

This hearty stew is the perfect meal for a cold winter's night.

INGREDIENTS

2 tbsp ghee

2 lbs venison stew meat (leg or shoulder)

1 onion, chopped

3 stalks celery, chopped

3 carrot sticks, peeled and sliced into ¼-inch rounds

4 cloves garlic, crushed

4 tomatoes, peeled and chopped

2 yams, chopped

1 bay leaf

½ tsp oregano

1 tsp thyme

3 cups beef broth

Salt and pepper just before serving

COOKING INSTRUCTIONS

› Heat 1 tablespoon of ghee in a heavy-bottomed pan over medium heat.

› Brown the venison on all sides for 5 minutes and place in the slow cooker.

› Lightly sauté the onion, celery, and carrots in the remaining ghee for 5 minutes or until the onion is translucent. Add the garlic and sauté until fragrant, about 3 minutes. Place mixture in the slow cooker.

› Add the rest of the ingredients and cook on low for 8 hours.

› Salt and pepper to taste, then serve.

SERVINGS: 6

POWERFUL PALEO **LIVER AND ONIONS WITH BACON**

Liver is really, really good for you. It's packed with vitamins. It has a rich flavor that turns some people off, but if you slow cook it and drench in caramelized onions and fragrant bacon, people's complaints turn into compliments.

INGREDIENTS

4 strips bacon, diced
2 medium onions, halved and sliced
3 cloves garlic, smashed
2 lbs beef liver, cubed
3 tomatoes, peeled and chopped
1 cup beef broth
1 tbsp dried parsley
Salt and pepper just before serving

COOKING INSTRUCTIONS

› In a heavy-bottomed pan, cook the bacon over medium heat until crisp and transfer to the slow cooker.

› Lightly sauté the onions in the remaining bacon grease over medium-low heat for 12 minutes, stirring frequently until onions are nicely caramelized. Add garlic and sauté until fragrant, about 3 minutes. Then transfer to the slow cooker.

› Turn the heat to medium high, and lightly sauté the liver for 5 minutes. Transfer to the slow cooker.

› Add tomatoes, broth and parsley to the slow cooker.

› Cook on low for 6-8 hours.

› Add salt and pepper to taste before serving.

SERVINGS: 6

BEEF ROAST WITH BEETS AND TARRAGON

This is a different take on a traditional roast that can last for many meals. The tarragon livens the flavor, while the beets are a nice alternative to potatoes and do well in the slow cooker.

INGREDIENTS

1 onion, chopped
3 tbsp butter
3-4 lbs chuck roast
8-10 beets, roots trimmed and peeled
4 tbsp chopped fresh tarragon
1 bay leaf
1 cup beef stock
Salt and pepper just before serving

COOKING INSTRUCTIONS

› Sauté the onion in a tablespoon of butter in a heavy-bottomed pan over medium heat for 5 minutes, until translucent.

› Transfer to the slow cooker.

› Turn the heat to medium high and brown the meat on all sides with remaining butter, about 8 minutes.

› Place the meat in the slow cooker with the remaining ingredients.

› Cook on low for 6-8 hours.

› Add salt and pepper to taste before serving.

SERVINGS: 6-8

PEPPERY **VENISON ROAST**

Pepper is a great complement to the rich and gamey flavors of venison. This traditional roast is the perfect special treat for a holiday.

INGREDIENTS

3 tbsp butter
2-3 lbs venison roast
1½ tbsp black peppercorns
2 onions, chopped
2 carrots, chopped
2 stalks celery, diced
3 cloves garlic, crushed
1 cup beef broth
1 tbsp dried parsley
½ tsp dried oregano
½ tsp dried basil
Salt just before serving

COOKING INSTRUCTIONS

› Heat a heavy-bottomed pan over medium-high heat. Add 1 tablespoon of the butter and brown the roast on all sides, about 8 minutes total.

› Transfer meat to the slow cooker.

› Turn the heat down to medium and melt the remaining butter.

› Crack the peppercorns with a mortar and pestle or by rolling over the corns with a wine bottle.

› Sauté the onions, carrots, celery and about one-third of the cracked pepper until the onions are translucent, about 5 minutes.

› Add the garlic and sauté another 3 minutes, until fragrant.

› Place mixture in slow cooker around the roast.

› Add the beef broth.

› Sprinkle in the parsley, oregano and basil, getting some on the roast and some in the sauce.

› Spread the remaining cracked pepper on the top of the roast.

› Cook on low for 6-8 hours.

› Salt to taste. Let rest for at least 10 minutes before carving and serving.

SERVINGS: 6-8

PART-TIME PALEO

I highly recommend that people give this whole Paleo thing a committed effort so you can experience the results for yourself. From my own experience and from talking to friends I have found that following Paleo part time is not as effective. Although some people experience some weight loss, many part-timers don't gain other major benefits like increased energy, feeling really healthy, and stabilization of moods. Different studies and books have suggested that gluten can stay in your system for a long time. This may be why cutting back, and not eliminating it altogether, doesn't give our bodies the opportunity to experience a surge in energy. Many of the foods that we are eliminating on the Paleo diet are inflammatory, so if we are still eating inflammatory foods regularly our bodies don't have as much of an opportunity to reduce the inflammation. With all that said, even if you are not fully committed, it is still better to go with the healthier option as often as possible!

WHY GRAINS, LENTILS, CHICKPEAS, SOY AND OTHER LEGUMES ARE NOT PART OF A PALEO LIFESTYLE

The foods that are not part of a Paleo lifestyle contain proteins and/or anti-nutrients that our bodies were not designed to handle. Grains contain large protein molecules called 'lectins.' The digestive system doesn't have the equipment necessary to break down lectins, which means they remain in your gut and cause irritation. These 'loose cannons' have the ability to bind to certain gut receptors and then act as keys, unlocking a gate that lets them out into our bodies. Unfortunately, lectins were born in a barn. They don't close the gate as they leave, and do damage to the gut on the way out. This is how the gut gets "leaky." That's not all!! Since lectins are not part of the normal environment, the body doesn't recognize them and the immune system, standing on guard, initiates an attack and creates antibodies against them. Those antibodies have a striking resemblance to other proteins normally found in our system. This leads to an autoimmune response (the body attacking itself). The story is similar for legumes and dairy. They also contain proteins, anti-nutrients and protease inhibitors that irritate the gut in much the same way as lectins.

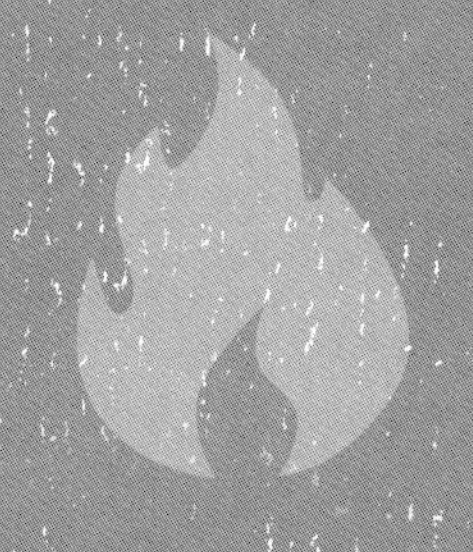

chapter three

SPICY AND TENDER LAMB FROM THE ANCIENT LANDS

LAMB CONSUMPTION IN THE U.S. IS FAIRLY LOW COMPARED TO OTHER COUNTRIES. However, lamb is a tasty meat to include in our diets, and it can add some variety. Maybe I am just biased because I grew up eating it. Lamb is a huge part of Armenian cuisine.

It is also a very healthy choice. Like cows, lambs are ruminant animals. Their natural diet consists of eating grass, therefore they are a good source of omega-3 fatty acids. Like beef, lamb is also a great source of healthy fats, iron, B vitamins and zinc.

PECAN-CRUSTED **RACK OF LAMB**

An impressive dish to serve to guests, it will bowl over people in both presentation and flavor. The mustard adds a nice tangy accent to the sweet-tasting pecans.

INGREDIENTS

1 cup pecans
¼ tsp rock salt
½ tsp pepper
1 tsp cumin
1 tsp smoked paprika
½ tsp honey
1 tbsp stone-ground mustard
Juice of ½ of lemon
1 rack of lamb
½ cup beef broth
1 sprig rosemary
Salt and pepper just before serving

COOKING INSTRUCTIONS

› Grind the pecans in a food processor or chop finely.

› Combine them with the salt, pepper, cumin and paprika to make the nut mixture.

› In a separate bowl, combine the honey, mustard and lemon juice.

› Brush lamb with the honey mixture, then coat with the nut mixture.

› Pour the broth into the slow cooker and then carefully add the rack of lamb.

› Put the sprig of rosemary next to the lamb and cook for 6-8 hours.

› Salt and pepper to taste and let rest for 5-10 minutes before serving.

SERVINGS: 4-5

BONELESS ROAST LEG OF LAMB WITH OLIVES AND MINT

The olives and mint give this dish a great and distinctive flavor. It's pretty easy to make, and an impressive dish to serve.

INGREDIENTS

1 tbsp ghee
2 lbs boneless leg of lamb roasts
2 cloves garlic, crushed
½ cup green olives
2 tbsp chopped fresh mint
1 tsp cumin
½ cup white wine
1 tsp fresh ground pepper
¼ tsp cayenne pepper
Salt and pepper just before serving

COOKING INSTRUCTIONS

› Preheat a heavy-bottomed pan to medium high.

› Add the ghee and brown the lamb roast on all sides, starting on the fat side, about 8 minutes.

› Transfer the meat to the slow cooker.

› Combine all other ingredients and pour over the meat.

› Cook on low for 8 hours.

SERVINGS: 4-6

LAMB WITH POMEGRANATE SAUCE

While this dish isn't the most elegant—the pomegranate juice turns things an odd color—the flavor is absolutely outstanding, and it is something nice and different.

INGREDIENTS

2 tbsp ghee
4 shallots, peeled and chopped
1 onion, chopped
2 cloves garlic, crushed
½ cup red wine
1 cup pomegranate juice
1 tbsp honey
3-4 lbs lamb chops
1 tsp chopped freshthyme
1 tsp chopped fresh tarragon
Salt and pepper just before serving

COOKING INSTRUCTIONS

› Melt ghee in a heavy-bottomed pan over medium heat.

› Sauté the shallots and onion until translucent, about 5 minutes.

› Add the garlic and cook another 3 minutes, until fragrant.

› Add the wine, pomegranate juice and honey and reduce for 5 minutes on medium low.

› Add the lamb to the slow cooker, pour the wine mixture over it and sprinkle with the thyme and tarragon.

› Cook on low for 6-8 hours.

› Salt and pepper to taste, then serve.

SERVINGS: 6-8

PERSIAN STEW WITH EGGPLANT

This is a dish my mom made for me a lot when I was growing up. The dish fills the house with great aromas; none of my childhood friends would refuse dinner if they could smell this cooking.

I want to throw in a quick reminder to always buy and cook with grass-fed meat. The flavor, particularly in lamb, is better and the meat has more nutrients. I try to get my lamb from local farmers, but you can often get grass-fed meats from your butcher.

INGREDIENTS

1 large onion, sliced
3 tbsp ghee
2 lbs lamb stew meat, cut into 1-inch cubes
4 cloves garlic, crushed
½ tsp turmeric, plus ¼ tsp turmeric
4 large tomatoes, peeled and chopped
2 tbsp tomato paste (preferably from a jar)
½ cup of beef broth
4 Japanese eggplants, peeled and halved lengthwise (if very large, cut into quarters)
Salt and pepper just before serving

COOKING INSTRUCTIONS

› Sauté the onion in 2 tablespoons of ghee melted in a heavy-bottomed pan over medium heat for 5 minutes, until translucent.

› Add the meat, garlic and ½ teaspoon turmeric. Brown the meat on all sides, about 6 minutes, being careful not to burn the garlic.

› Add tomatoes and tomato paste, and sauté for a few more minutes

› Transfer all ingredients from the pan, including any juices in the pan, to the slow cooker.

› Add broth to the slow cooker.

› Heat remaining tablespoon of ghee in the same pan over medium heat, and sauté the eggplants until browned on both sides.

› Lay eggplants on top of the meat in the slow cooker. Do not mix. The eggplants seem large in this dish, but with 6 hours of slow cooking, the eggplants caramelize and mix in with the stew.

› Cook on low for 6 hours.

› Add remaining ¼ teaspoon of turmeric to the slow cooker.

› Salt and pepper to taste, then serve.

SERVINGS: 6-8

WHITE WINE **LAMB CHOPS**

These delicious and decadent little chops are a real crowd-pleaser.

INGREDIENTS

2 tbsp ghee
2 lbs lamb chops
1 onion, chopped
2 cloves garlic, crushed
1 cup dry white wine
2 tomatoes, coarsely chopped
1 tsp cumin
½ tsp paprika
½ tsp dried thyme
¼ tsp cayenne pepper
Salt and pepper just before serving

COOKING INSTRUCTIONS

› In a large heavy-bottomed pan, melt 1 tablespoon of ghee over medium heat and brown the lamb in batches. Then transfer to the slow cooker.

› Sauté the onion in the remaining ghee until translucent.

› Add the garlic and cook for another 3 minutes, until fragrant. Transfer onion mixture to the slow cooker.

› Add the wine and tomatoes to the slow cooker.

› Use a spoon to sprinkle in the spices, spreading them evenly over the lamb and sauce.

› Cook on low for 6 hours.

› Salt and pepper to taste before serving.

SERVINGS: 4-6

ARMENIAN **LAMB AND APRICOT STEW**

Armenians use a lot of lamb in their cooking, and they often incorporate fruit and nuts. Here the apricots add a nice sweet flavor to balance the spiciness of the dish.

INGREDIENTS

2 tbsp coconut oil
1 onion, thinly sliced
2 cloves garlic, crushed
1 tbsp grated fresh ginger
2 chili peppers, chopped
6 oz dried apricots
2 lbs lamb stew meat, cut into 1-inch cubes
3 sweet potatoes, peeled and cubed
2 cups beef broth
1 tbsp fresh lemon juice
¼ cup brandy (optional)
1 tsp dried basil
1 tsp dried dill
1 tbsp dried parsley
Salt and pepper just before serving

COOKING INSTRUCTIONS

- Melt 1 tablespoon coconut oil in a heavy-bottomed pan over medium heat. Lightly sauté the onion for about 3 minutes, then add the garlic, ginger, chili peppers and apricots, and cook another 3 minutes.
- Transfer mixture to the slow cooker.
- Melt the remaining coconut oil in the pan, and brown the lamb in batches, about 6 minutes a batch, then transfer to the slow cooker. (Note that it takes longer to brown in coconut oil.)
- Add sweet potatoes to the slow cooker.
- Mix the broth, lemon juice, brandy (if using) and dried herbs in a bowl, and pour over the meat in the slow cooker.
- Cook on low for 6-8 hours.
- Salt and pepper to taste, then serve.

SERVINGS: 4-6

LAMB AND CUMIN CASSEROLE

Armenian markets are known for their great fresh meat, and this Paleo-take on a traditional dish tastes that much better when you use freshly butchered, grass-fed lamb.

INGREDIENTS

2 lbs lamb stew meat, cubed
2 tbsp butter
1 onion, sliced
1 bell pepper, chopped
2 carrots, sliced
3 cloves garlic, chopped
2 tsp cumin
1 tsp allspice
2 tbsp tomato paste
2 sweet potatoes, sliced
4 tomatoes, peeled and chopped
½ cup beef broth
Salt and pepper just before serving

COOKING INSTRUCTIONS

› Brown the lamb in 1 tablespoon of butter in a heavy-bottomed pan over medium heat, about 5 minutes, and transfer to the slow cooker.

› Sauté the onion, bell pepper and carrots until the onion is translucent, about 5 minutes.

› Add the garlic, spices and tomato paste, and cook for another 3 minutes, until fragrant. Transfer the mixture to the slow cooker.

› Add the tomatoes to the slow cooker along with the broth and cook for 3 hours.

› Add sweet potatoes and cook on low for 3-4 hours.

› Salt and pepper to taste, then serve.

SERVINGS: 6

INDIAN **LAMB**

I love Indian food because of its distinctive flavors. Here the coconut milk not only adds a richness, but is also a good source of fat and a Paleo Diet favorite. Note that this dish requires marinating so it's best to start preparations the day before.

INGREDIENTS

1 tbsp grated ginger
2 cloves garlic, minced
1 tbsp chopped fresh mint
1 tbsp chopped fresh cilantro
1 tsp coriander
1 tsp garam masala
½ tsp turmeric
½ tsp salt
Juice from ½ of lemon
1 onion, chopped
2 fresh red chilies, chopped
2 lbs lamb, cubed
1 cup coconut milk
Salt and pepper just before serving

COOKING INSTRUCTIONS

› Mix all the ingredients except the lamb and coconut milk in a large bowl. Coat the lamb with the spice mixture, then let it marinate for at least 3 hours, but preferably overnight.

› Place the lamb with the marinade and the coconut milk in the slow cooker, and cook on low for 6-8 hours

› Salt and pepper to taste, then serve.

SERVINGS: 4-6

HARISSA-BRAISED **LAMB SHANKS**

This is a spicy dish, so beware, the faint of heart. But be rewarded, those who like strong flavors. Harissa paste comes from North Africa and is made from hot peppers and garlic and available in most gourmet food stores.

INGREDIENTS

1 tbsp ghee
1 tsp cumin
1 tsp coriander
1 tsp smoked paprika
3 lbs lamb shanks (make sure they fit into your slow cooker)
¼ tsp allspice
4 cloves garlic, crushed
12 shallots, peeled and whole
8 tomatoes, peeled and chopped or 1 can chopped tomatoes
1 cup chicken stock
1 tbsp Harissa paste (use 2 tbsp if you want more heat)
Salt and pepper just before serving

COOKING INSTRUCTIONS

› Soften the ghee in the microwave, then mix with the cumin, coriander and paprika. Rub onto the lamb shanks.

› Brown the shanks in a broiler for about 2 minutes a side, being careful not to burn them, and transfer to the slow cooker.

› Combine the rest of the ingredients in a bowl, and pour over the shanks into the slow cooker. Cook for 6-8 hours.

› Salt and pepper to taste, then serve.

SERVINGS: 6

GROUND LAMB
WITH PINE NUTS AND MINT

Ground meat is an affordable way to include pasture-raised meat in your diet. This is a really tasty and easy recipe. The pine nuts and mint give a nice light and satisfying flavor.

INGREDIENTS

2 onions, chopped
1 green pepper, chopped
⅛ cup pine nuts
1 tbsp ghee
3 cloves garlic, crushed
2 lbs ground lamb
1 tsp cumin
1 tsp paprika
¼ cup finely chopped fresh mint
Salt and pepper just before serving

COOKING INSTRUCTIONS

› Sauté the onions, green pepper and pine nuts in the ghee in a heavy-bottomed pan over medium heat for 5 minutes, until the onions are translucent.

› Add the garlic and cook another 3 minutes, until fragrant.

› Combine the lamb with the cumin and paprika and brown with the onions, breaking up the meat with a wooden spoon, about 8 minutes.

› Transfer lamb mixture to the slow cooker.

› Cook on low for 4 hours or on high for 2 hours.

› Add chopped mint 20 minutes before serving.

› Salt and pepper to taste, then serve.

SERVINGS: 4-6

LAMB TAGINE

Strong Moroccan flavors make this dish exotic and delicious.
It warms me up on a cold winter's night.

INGREDIENTS

2 lbs lamb stew meat, cut into 1½-inch cubes
2 tbsp ghee
1 medium onion, chopped
3 cloves garlic, crushed
2 tsp paprika
¼ tsp turmeric
1 tsp cumin
¼ tsp cayenne pepper
1 tsp cinnamon
¼ tsp ground cloves
½ tsp ground cardamom
½ tsp coriander
6 tomatoes, peeled and chopped
1 cup chicken stock
Juice of 1 lemon
1 small butternut squash, peeled and chopped
Salt and pepper just before serving

COOKING INSTRUCTIONS

› In a heavy-bottomed pan over medium heat, brown the lamb in 1 tablespoon of ghee in batches, about 5 minutes a batch.

› Transfer the meat to the slow cooker.

› Add the remaining ghee to the pan and sauté the onion until translucent.

› Add the garlic and cook another 3 minutes, until fragrant.

› Place all the ingredients except butternut squash into the slow cooker and cook for 6-8 hours.

› Add the butternut squash for the last 3 hours to avoid overcooking.

› Salt and pepper to taste, then serve.

SERVINGS: 6

POST-WORKOUT NUTRITION

Post-workout nutrition protocol depends on several factors; the individual's goals (body composition, performance, health), the type/length/intensity of training, health status and body's response/needs. For those looking to lose weight or lean out with performance playing second fiddle, post workout carbs may not be necessary.

POST-WORKOUT NUTRITION GOALS

1. Maintain and Restore Muscle Glycogen

    - Replenishment is most successful in the post workout period.
    - Plant-based carbohydrates are optimal, including: yams, sweet potatoes, squash, plantains, taro, yucca, cassava, white potatoes with the skin removed, rutabaga, other roots and tubers, bananas, and other fruit.
    - Liquid nutrition like shakes, powders, and other protein supplements should not be relied on. Real food is always the best option!

2. Prevent Muscle Breakdown that Occurs with Exercise

    - Replenishment is most important in the post workout period to reverse muscle catabolism immediately resulting in reduced recovery time and higher workout intensity in the next session.
    - High quality animal-sourced protein is the best choice as it provides the branched chain amino acids (BCAAs) that are key in muscle recovery.

chapter four

PERFECT PORK:
SUCCULENT FROM THE SLOW COOKER

UNLIKE WITH LAMB OR BEEF, IT IS A BIT MORE DIFFICULT TO VERIFY THE DIET OF A PIG SINCE PIGS EAT PRETTY MUCH ANYTHING. Wild pigs have to forage for their food and since they are omnivores, they eat insects, worms, fruits and flowers. Domesticated pigs, even organic ones, are usually given feed from corn, wheat or other grains. However, there are ranchers who raise their pigs on farm scraps and pasture, those are the ones to eat if you can find them.

Pork is a good source of protein. Studies have also shown it to be a good source of vitamins and minerals, such as selenium, thiamin, zinc and B vitamins. Plus, who doesn't love bacon!

I particularly like cooking with pork because it seems to go really well with fruit, and I love incorporating fruit into a main dish.

PEAR GINGER **PORK CHOPS**

I love coming home and smelling the fall flavors in this dish. The ginger adds a nice accent. The pork chops come out succulent and tender.

INGREDIENTS

2 tbsp coconut oil
4 thick-cut pork chops
2 ripe d'anjou pears, cored and cut into chunks
1 tbsp minced ginger
2 tbsp apple cider vinegar
1 cup white wine (or substitute water or broth)
½ tsp cinnamon
1 tsp allspice
2 tbsp honey
Salt and pepper just before serving

COOKING INSTRUCTIONS

- Melt 1 tablespoon of the coconut oil in a heavy-bottomed pan over medium heat.
- Brown the pork chops on both sides (in batches, if necessary) for about 5 minutes total, then place in the slow cooker.
- Sauté the pears and ginger in the remaining coconut oil.
- Add the vinegar and wine, turn heat to medium low and cook for 5 minutes to reduce slightly.
- Add the cinnamon, allspice and honey to the pan and stir to combine.
- Pour mixture over chops in slow cooker.
- Cook on low for 6 hours.
- Salt and pepper to taste, then serve.

SERVINGS: 4

SPICY PORK TENDERLOIN STUFFED WITH PRUNES

The prunes and jalapeños give this dish a great sweet and spicy flavor combination. I recommend you eat this dish fresh from the slow cooker because the prunes can get mushy and make the sauce heavy overnight.

INGREDIENTS

2 lbs pork tenderloin
½ tsp black pepper
1 tsp chili powder
1 tsp thyme
1 tsp sage
1 onion, quartered
2 cloves garlic, crushed
2 jalapeño peppers, cut into strips
2 tbsp coconut oil
1 cup prunes, pitted and chopped
¼ cup brandy
½ cup chicken broth
2 bay leaves
Salt and pepper just before serving

COOKING INSTRUCTIONS

› Rub the tenderloin with pepper, chili powder, thyme and sage and reserve any extra herbs.

› Sauté the onion, garlic and jalapeños in 1 tablespoon of the coconut oil in a heavy-bottomed pan over medium heat for 5 minutes. Transfer to the slow cooker.

› Brown the pork in the remaining coconut oil for about 5 minutes and set aside.

› Turn the heat down to medium low and simmer the prunes in the brandy for 5 minutes.

› Create an incision in the pork, and stuff some of the brandied prunes inside along with the sauce. Place the remaining prune mixture in the slow cooker along with the meat.

› Add the broth, bay leaves and remaining herbs.

› Cook on low 4-6 hours.

› Salt and pepper to taste, then serve.

SERVINGS: 4

APPLE CIDER PORK WITH ROSEMARY

This is another nice fall pork dish that will fill your house with great aromas. Note that often supermarket pork won't taste different than the organic variety. However, organic pork doesn't contain antibiotics so I'd recommend spending money on the organic brands. It's also very important to buy organic apples to avoid the pesticides as well as get better flavor.

INGREDIENTS

3 lbs pork roast
2 tbsp coconut oil
1 onion, chopped
2 cloves garlic, crushed
2 apples, peeled, cored and chopped
2 cups hard apple cider
1 tbsp minced fresh rosemary
1 tsp minced fresh thyme
Salt and pepper just before serving

COOKING INSTRUCTIONS

› Brown the pork in 1 tablespoon of coconut oil in a heavy-bottomed pan over medium-high heat for about 8 minutes. Transfer to the slow cooker.

› Turn the heat down to medium and sauté the onion in the remaining coconut oil for about 5 minutes.

› Add the garlic and apples, cook for another 3 minutes, and then transfer the mixture to the slow cooker.

› Add all the other ingredients and cook on low for 6-8 hours.

› Salt and pepper to taste, then serve.

SERVINGS: 6

ROASTED **CITRUS PORK**

Can you tell that I love pairing pork with fruit flavors? This dish is more sour than sweet which makes it a bit different than the others.

INGREDIENTS

3 tbsp coconut oil
3-4 lbs pork roast
4 whole cloves
3 cloves garlic, crushed
1 tsp orange zest
1 tsp lemon zest
Juice of 1 lemon
½ cup fresh-squeezed orange juice
¼ cup white wine
½ tsp thyme
Salt and pepper just before serving

COOKING INSTRUCTIONS

› Melt 1 tablespoon of coconut oil in a heavy-bottomed pan over medium-high heat and brown the pork on all sides for about 8 minutes.

› Turn the heat down to medium. While the pan cools slightly, poke four whole cloves into the top of the roast, evenly spaced, then transfer to the slow cooker.

› Sauté the garlic in the remaining coconut oil for 3 minutes, until fragrant, being careful not to burn the coconut oil or garlic, and transfer to the slow cooker.

› Combine the zests, juices, white wine and thyme in a bowl, then pour over the roast and cook on low for 6 hours.

› Salt and pepper to taste, then serve.

SERVINGS: 6-8

PORK CHOPS IN FIG SAUCE

Figs remind me of my childhood. Almost every Armenian family makes fig jam. Now that I don't incorporate a lot of sugar into my diet, I skip the jam and get my fig fix from dishes like this.

INGREDIENTS

1 tbsp coconut oil
4 thick-cut pork chops
½ cup chicken broth or dry white wine
2 tsp apple cider vinegar
¼ cup finely chopped dried figs
1 tbsp honey
½ tsp chopped fresh thyme
½ tsp chopped fresh sage
Salt and pepper just before serving

COOKING INSTRUCTIONS

› Heat the coconut oil in a heavy-bottomed pan over medium heat.

› Brown the pork chops in batches, about 5 minutes a batch, and transfer to the slow cooker.

› Add the remaining ingredients to the slow cooker, making sure to stir in the honey so it's well incorporated.

› Cook on low for 4-6 hours.

› Salt and pepper to taste, then serve

SERVINGS: 4

PORK WITH PINEAPPLE AND PEPPERS

This is a great summertime special the whole family will love.

INGREDIENTS

2 tbsp coconut oil

3 lbs pork roast, cut into 1½-inch cubes

½ white onion, diced

3 cloves garlic, crushed

2 jalapeño peppers, diced

2 cups fresh-cut pineapple

2 tbsp apple cider vinegar

½ cup dry white wine

Salt and pepper just before serving

COOKING INSTRUCTIONS

› Melt 1 tablespoon of coconut oil in a heavy-bottomed pan over medium-high heat and brown the pork in batches, about 6 minutes a batch. Transfer to the slow cooker.

› Turn the heat down to medium and sauté the onion in the remaining coconut oil for 5 minutes.

› Add the garlic and peppers, and cook for another 3 minutes.

› Transfer the mixture to the slow cooker. Combine the pineapple, vinegar and white wine in a bowl, then transfer to the slow cooker and cook on low for 6 hours.

› Salt and pepper to taste, then serve.

SERVINGS: 6

DIJON **HAM**

Great for a holiday family meal, this dish is really easy and keeps the oven free to make other holiday delights. It also makes great leftovers. Wrapping a piece in butter lettuce with some of the sauce makes a perfect sandwich. We often eat it for breakfast. It's a versatile dish.

INGREDIENTS

5-6 lbs ham
¼ cup apple cider vinegar
¼ cup honey
¼ cup coconut oil
1 tsp thyme
2 tbsp Dijon mustard
Zest of 1 orange
Pepper just before serving

COOKING INSTRUCTIONS

› Put the ham in the slow cooker.

› Combine the rest of the ingredients in a large bowl, making sure the honey and mustard are both well incorporated.

› Pour the sauce over the ham in the slow cooker.

› Cook on low for 6 hours.

› Pepper to taste, then serve.

SERVINGS: 8-10

PORK RIBS IN MANGO BBQ SAUCE

Many tropical fruits like mangos are high in sugar so I don't eat them too much. In this case, incorporating them into an entrée is a good way to satisfy your mango craving since a little goes a long way.

INGREDIENTS

½ onion, minced
1 tbsp grated fresh ginger
2 cloves garlic, chopped
2 tsp ground mustard
1 red chili, seeded and finely chopped
2 tsp paprika
1 tbsp tomato paste
½ cup apple cider vinegar
Juice of 1 orange
Pinch of ground cloves
1 tbsp honey
1 cup tomato puree
½ cup chicken broth
3-4 lbs pork ribs
2 cups fresh mango, peeled and diced
Salt and pepper just before serving

COOKING INSTRUCTIONS

› Mix all the ingredients except the ribs and mango in a bowl, making sure the honey, mustard and tomato are mostly incorporated.

› Cut ribs into serving sizes or pieces that will fit your slow cooker (two or three rib sections will probably work).

› Place ribs in the slow cooker and pour the sauce over them.

› Cook on low for 4-5 hours. Be sure not to overcook, or the meat will fall off the bone.

› Remove carefully, salt and pepper to taste, then serve.

SERVINGS: 4-6

ASIAN PORK
WITH COCONUT AMINOS

Coconut aminos sounds like a biology term rather than a delicious food. Don't be turned off; it's a good substitute for its soy-based and often wheat-packed brethren, and it delivers nice flavor in this Eastern-inspired dish.

INGREDIENTS

2 tbsp coconut oil
2 lbs boneless pork shoulder, cut into chunks
4 shallots, minced
4 cloves garlic, crushed
3-4 red chilies, sliced
1 tsp dried shrimp paste
¼ cup coconut aminos
2 tsp honey
1 tbsp lime juice
½ cup chicken broth
Pepper just before serving

COOKING INSTRUCTIONS

› Melt 1 tablespoon coconut oil in a heavy-bottomed pan over medium heat.

› Brown the pork in batches, about 5 minutes a batch, and transfer to the slow cooker.

› Sauté the shallots in the remaining coconut oil, about 5 minutes.

› Add the garlic and chilies, cook another 3 minutes, and transfer the mixture to the slow cooker.

› Add the rest of the ingredients to the slow cooker and cook on low for 4-6 hours.

› Pepper to taste, then serve.

SERVINGS: 4-6

ASIAN-INSPIRED **RIBS**

My husband thinks this is the best dish I've ever made in a slow cooker. He loves what the five-spice powder brings to the dish, adding a powerful flavor without overwhelming it.

INGREDIENTS

1 rack of pork ribs (about 12 ribs)
½ cup Tamari or coconut aminos
½ cup raw honey
2 tbsp coconut vinegar
1 tsp five-spice powder
½ tbsp grated fresh ginger
3 cloves garlic, crushed
Juice of 1 lime
Pinch of red pepper flakes
1 tbsp sesame oil 10 minutes before serving
Salt and pepper just before serving

COOKING INSTRUCTIONS

- Cut rack into individual ribs and place in the slow cooker.
- Mix together all ingredients except sesame oil and pour over ribs.
- Cook on low for 4-5 hours. Be sure not to overcook, or the meat will fall off the bone.
- Add the sesame oil 10 minutes before serving.
- Salt and pepper to taste, then serve.

SERVINGS: 4-5

PORK GOULASH RECIPE

Goulash is a traditional Hungarian stew that is nice and hearty and an international favorite of mine.

INGREDIENTS

2 lbs pork roast, cut into cubes
1 tbsp caraway seeds
2 tbsp sweet Hungarian paprika
2 slices bacon, diced
1 onion, chopped
3 cloves garlic, crushed
2 tbsp apple cider vinegar
2 cups sauerkraut, without liquid
4 tomatoes, peeled and chopped
2 cups chicken broth
Salt and pepper just before serving

COOKING INSTRUCTIONS

› Toss pork with caraway seeds and 1 tablespoon of paprika.

› Cook bacon in a large heavy-bottomed pan over medium heat until crispy, about 5 minutes, and reserve.

› Brown pork in bacon fat in batches, about 5 minutes a batch, and transfer to the slow cooker with a slotted spoon.

› Add the rest of the ingredients to the slow cooker and cook on low for 6-8 hours.

› Salt and pepper to taste, top with bacon, then serve.

SERVINGS: 4-6

SPICY **SAUSAGE AND PEPPER STEW**

This hearty and delicious dish is easy to make and a great one to pop into the slow cooker when you are busy.

INGREDIENTS

1½-2 lbs spicy Italian sausage, sliced into ¼-inch coins

1 tsp ghee

1 onion, sliced

3 cloves garlic, crushed

2 bell peppers, chopped (I usually use 1 green and 1 red)

8 tomatoes, blanched and peeled or 1 (14-oz) can stewed tomatoes

2 cups chicken broth

½ tsp dried oregano

½ tsp dried thyme

Salt and pepper just before serving

COOKING INSTRUCTIONS

› Brown the sausage in batches in a heavy-bottomed pan over medium heat, about 5 minutes a batch.

› Add the ghee and sauté the onion until translucent, about 5 minutes.

› Add the garlic and bell peppers, cook another 3 minutes, then transfer the whole mixture to the slow cooker with the rest of the ingredients.

› Cook on low for 5-6 hours.

› Salt and pepper to taste, then serve.

SERVINGS: 6-8

PORK AND **CABBAGE SOUP**

This is a hearty winter recipe. The bacon gives the dish the nice smoky flavor I love.

INGREDIENTS

3 strips bacon, diced
1 lb pork loin, cubed
1 tbsp ghee
1 onion, chopped
2 carrots, sliced
2 parsnips, chopped
2-3 cloves garlic, crushed
½ medium head of cabbage, shredded
4 cups chicken or beef broth
6 tomatoes, chopped
1 bay leaf
1 tbsp gluten-free Worcestershire sauce
½ tsp basil
½ tsp oregano
Salt and pepper just before serving

COOKING INSTRUCTIONS

› Cook bacon in a heavy-bottomed pan over medium heat until crispy, about 5 minutes, and reserve for garnish.

› Brown pork in the bacon grease in batches, about 5 minutes a batch, and transfer to the slow cooker.

› Melt the ghee and sauté the onion, carrots and parsnips for 5 minutes, until the onion is translucent.

› Add the garlic, cook another 3 minutes and transfer the mixture to the slow cooker.

› Add the rest of the ingredients to the slow cooker and cook on low for 6-8 hours.

› Salt and pepper to taste.

› Garnish with bacon bits, then serve.

SERVINGS: 6

SLIGHTLY SPICY **CARNITAS**

We serve this at our house a lot. We use it throughout the week for other dishes, from lunchtime lettuce-wrap sandwiches to dinner over steamed vegetables.

INGREDIENTS

1 tsp sea salt
1 tbsp cumin
½ tsp oregano
1 tbsp coriander
1 tsp paprika
½ tsp cayenne pepper
3 lbs boneless pork shoulder, cut into 4 large chunks
2 tbsp ghee
1 onion, diced
4 cloves garlic, crushed
1 jalapeno, minced
¼ cup chicken broth
2 bay leaves
Salt and pepper just before serving

COOKING INSTRUCTIONS

› Combine the salt, cumin, oregano, coriander, paprika and cayenne in a bowl. Rub over the pork, reserving the extra spices (and being careful not to touch your eyes).

› Melt 1 tablespoon of the ghee in a heavy-bottomed pan over medium heat. Brown the pork in batches, about 5 minutes a batch, and transfer to the slow cooker.

› Sauté the onion in the remaining ghee until translucent, about 5 minutes.

› Add the garlic and jalapeño pepper, cook another 3 minutes, then transfer the mixture to the slow cooker.

› Add the chicken broth and bay leaves to the slow cooker, and cook on low for 5-6 hours.

› Pull the meat apart with 2 forks and cook for an additional hour.

› Salt and pepper to taste, then serve.

SERVINGS: 8

SLOW-COOKER **STUFFING**

I made this for Thanksgiving, and it was a hit with my non-Paleo in-laws. The flavors worked well together and you won't miss the starch. It also saves a spot in the oven, a win-win.

INGREDIENTS

3 Italian sausages, removed from casing (I use 2 hot and 1 mild)
2 tbsp ghee
2 cups mushrooms, sliced
½ yellow onion, diced
2 stalks celery, diced (about ¾ cup)
3 cloves garlic, crushed
1 Granny Smith apple, peeled and diced
2 yams, peeled and chopped
6 fresh sage leaves, minced
½ cup chopped pecans
¼ cup dried cranberries
1 cup beef stock
Salt and pepper just before serving

COOKING INSTRUCTIONS

› Brown the sausage in a heavy-bottomed pan over medium heat, breaking up the meat as it cooks, and transfer to the slow cooker.

› Turn heat to low and melt the ghee.

› Add the rest of the dry ingredients to the slow cooker, pour the melted ghee over it and mix with a wooden spoon.

› Add the stock and cook on low for 3-4 hours.

› Salt and pepper to taste, then serve.

SERVINGS: 6-8

INSULIN SENSITIVITY & PALEO

Today's Standard American Diet is a high-carb sugar-laden nightmare. The heavy carb and sugar load results in high levels of glucose in the blood. This requires the pancreas to make and secrete more insulin, which results in high insulin levels in the blood. When insulin levels are high, inflammation increases and insulin sensitivity decreases. The longer these conditions exist the less "sensitive" our cells become to insulin (think tolerance, like with drugs and alcohol) and the more insulin it requires to get the sugar out of the blood and into the cells. This contributes to further inflammation and even less insulin sensitivity. We've now created a state of insulin resistance. There are other factors that increase inflammation and contribute to insulin resistance; sleep, stress, overall diet composition (grains, dairy, fat type, etc), among other factors all play major roles in the process.

The Paleo diet, when followed correctly, minimizes many of the dietary causes of inflammation and helps to improve the insulin-resistant state. Keep in mind that if the Paleo diet is not implemented correctly and is a diet high in Paleo "treats" like dried fruit, nuts, smoothies and fruit, the improvements in insulin sensitivity will be drastically reduced. Additionally the Paleo lifestyle calls for smart "not over the top" exercise, adequate and quality sleep, stress reduction and other habits that encourage an anti-inflammatory environment therefore decreasing insulin resistance and increasing insulin sensitivity.

It is often said that certain spices and foods may help increase insulin sensitivity. Cinnamon is one of these magic foods. Several studies have shown that the polyphenols in cinnamon may act as insulin sensitizers. Many of these studies have been conducted in rats and there are few well-controlled, human clinical studies that have been done. This makes it difficult to make a solid conclusion of cinnamon's efficacy as an insulin sensitizer. The research that is available is positive, but at this point inconclusive. Is it worth a shot? It definitely will not hurt you and if you add it to your recipes it's very tasty!

chapter five

SLOW-COOKED **CHICKEN FAVORITES AND OTHER FEATHERED FRIENDS**

IT CAN BE DIFFICULT TO VERIFY A CHICKEN'S DIET, as organic and non-organic chickens are often both raised on feed. Organic is always a better option, as organic feed and organic chickens do not contain antibiotics, pesticides, and chemical fertilizers. There are also farmers who put great effort into varying the diets of their chickens with farm scraps, insects and pasture feeding. Pasture-raised chickens have better omega-3 to omega-6 composition, and so do their eggs. If you have access to pasture-raised chicken and eggs from local farmers, this is the best Paleo way to go.

Chicken is a good source of protein, some B vitamins, selenium and choline. It's another protein that goes well with lots of different ingredients, including nuts, fruit and different herbs.

GARLIC TARRAGON **CHICKEN**

I love tarragon and it adds a different twist to a traditional chicken dish. The butter and tons of garlic makes a great basting sauce that I pour over the chicken just before serving, but if you don't tolerate butter well, you should try the Slow-Cooker Chicken Pesto instead, page 142.

INGREDIENTS

1 whole chicken, cut into breasts, whole legs and wings, skin removed

1 stick of butter

3 tbsp minced fresh tarragon

1 whole head of garlic, peeled and minced

½ cup chicken stock

Salt and pepper just before serving

COOKING INSTRUCTIONS

- Brown the chicken in batches in 1 tablespoon of the butter in a heavy-bottomed pan over medium-high heat, about 5 minutes a batch.
- Mix the tarragon with 1 tablespoon butter softened in the microwave and 1 teaspoon minced garlic.
- Rub this all over the chicken parts and place them in the slow cooker with the chicken stock and remaining garlic and butter.
- Cook on low for 4-5 hours.
- Salt and pepper to taste. Pour sauce over the chicken, then serve.

SERVINGS: 6

CHICKEN WITH BUTTERNUT SQUASH AND FIGS

Butternut squash is another one of those foods that I started preparing once I adopted a Paleo diet and became much more adventurous in cooking new vegetables. When I'm working out a lot, I try to include more carbs in my diet and butternut squash is one of my favorites. In this dish, I love how the sweetness of the squash and figs complement the pungent rosemary. If you prefer your butternut squash more crunchy, add it half way through cooking time.

INGREDIENTS

2 tbsp coconut oil
1 onion, diced
3 cloves garlic, crushed
3 lbs skinless chicken breasts or boneless thighs
½ cup dried figs
½ butternut squash, peeled and cubed
1 cup chicken broth
1 tbsp chopped fresh rosemary
1 tsp chopped fresh tarragon
1 tsp chopped fresh sage
Salt and pepper just before serving

COOKING INSTRUCTIONS

- In a heavy-bottomed pan, melt the coconut oil and sauté the onion over medium heat for 5 minutes, until translucent.
- Add the garlic and cook for another minute, until fragrant.
- Add the chicken in batches and brown for 5 minutes a batch, removing the onion and garlic with the first batch, and transfer to the slow cooker.
- Add the figs, squash, broth and herbs to the slow cooker.
- Cook on low for 6 hours.
- Salt and pepper to taste, then serve.

SERVINGS: 6

CHICKEN WITH MUSHROOMS AND ARTICHOKES

This is a simple and savory dinner. The combination sounds gourmet while the dish is easy to make.

INGREDIENTS

3 lbs skinless chicken parts (breasts, thighs or any part of choice)
½ tsp paprika
3 tbsp butter
½ onion, chopped
1 cup mushrooms, halved
1 (16-oz) jar artichoke hearts, drained
½ tsp dried thyme
½ cup dry white wine
½ cup chicken broth
Salt and pepper just before serving

COOKING INSTRUCTIONS

- Coat the chicken with the paprika.
- Melt the 2 tablespoons of the butter in a heavy-bottomed pan over medium heat. Brown the chicken in batches on all sides, about 5 minutes a batch, and transfer to the slow cooker.
- Melt the remaining butter in the pan and sauté the onion for 5 minutes, until translucent.
- Add the mushrooms and artichokes and cook another 5-8 minutes, until the mushrooms are slightly browned, then transfer the mixture to the slow cooker.
- Combine the thyme, wine and broth in a bowl, then pour over the chicken in the slow cooker and cook on low for 6 hours.
- Salt and pepper to taste, then serve.

SERVINGS: 6

CHICKEN WITH GINGER AND LEMON

This recipe is a mix of all my favorite ingredients. The zesty flavors pack quite a punch.

INGREDIENTS

½ tsp cinnamon
1 tsp cumin
¼ tsp turmeric
3 lbs skinless chicken parts (breasts, thighs, or any part of choice)
3 tbsp ghee
1 onion, thinly sliced
3 cloves garlic, crushed
¼ cup grated fresh ginger
¼ cup dried cranberries
2 strands of saffron
Juice of 1 lemon
Zest of 1 lemon
½ cup chicken stock
2 tomatoes, coarsely chopped
Salt and pepper just before serving

COOKING INSTRUCTIONS

› Mix cinnamon, cumin and turmeric in a bowl and toss chicken to coat.

› In a heavy-bottomed pan over medium heat, melt 1 tablespoon of ghee and sauté the onion and garlic until onion is translucent, about 5 minutes. Transfer to the slow cooker.

› Melt the remaining ghee in the pan and add the chicken. Brown on both sides in batches for about 5 minutes a batch.

› Transfer the chicken and remaining ghee to the slow cooker.

› Combine the rest of the ingredients in a bowl, then transfer to the slow cooker and cook on low for 4-6 hours.

› Salt and pepper to taste, then serve.

SERVINGS: 6

CHICKEN BREASTS STUFFED WITH SUN-DRIED TOMATOES

The already intense flavor of sun-dried tomatoes allows you to make a tasty, yet quick, dish, without having to add too many ingredients. Recipes like this are a must in our house since we both work full-time, have very busy schedules, but love to enjoy delicious homemade meals.

INGREDIENTS

1 tbsp ghee
½ onion, chopped
3 cloves garlic, crushed
3 lbs skinless chicken breasts
1 (8-oz) jar sun-dried tomatoes
½ cup chicken broth
2 tsp dried oregano
½ tsp dried basil
Salt and pepper just before serving

COOKING INSTRUCTIONS

› In a heavy-bottomed pan over medium heat, melt the ghee and sauté the onion and garlic until onion is translucent, about 5 minutes.

› Meanwhile, cut a big pocket in each chicken breast.

› Spoon the onion and garlic into each pocket and follow with 2-3 dried tomatoes. Carefully transfer stuffed breasts into the slow cooker.

› Add the broth and sprinkle the herbs over the top.

› Cook on low for 4-6 hours.

› Salt and pepper to taste, then serve.

SERVINGS: 6

HERBED CHICKEN WITH LEMON

Chicken with lemon and herbs is a classic for a reason. It's just great; we cook it all the time. It has a nice light flavor, and is great reheated for easy lunches or dinners during the week. The flavors are basic and not overpowering.

INGREDIENTS

3 tbsp ghee
3 lbs skinless chicken legs and thighs or whole chicken cut up
1 medium onion, chopped
3 cloves garlic, crushed
2 tbsp red wine vinegar
Juice of 1 lemon
1 cup chicken broth
Zest of 1 lemon
1 tbsp chopped fresh rosemary
½ tsp dried oregano
½ tsp dried thyme

COOKING INSTRUCTIONS

› Melt 1 tablespoon of ghee in a heavy-bottomed pan over medium heat.

› Brown the chicken in batches, about 5 minutes a batch, and transfer to the slow cooker.

› Melt the remaining ghee in the pan and sauté the onion for 5 minutes, until translucent.

› Add the garlic, cook another 3 minutes, and transfer mixture to the slow cooker.

› Pour the remaining liquids over the chicken and sprinkle the zest and herbs all over the top.

› Cook on low for 4-6 hours.

› Salt and pepper to taste, then serve.

SERVINGS: 6

HONEY **CHICKEN THIGHS**

Growing up I used to go to a restaurant called Rocky Cola Café in our little suburb of Los Angeles. I had many fun times with friends while eating chicken tenders with a honey-mustard dipping sauce. This recipe is inspired by my many memories, but is a much healthier version.

INGREDIENTS

1 tbsp coconut oil
8 skinless and boneless chicken thighs
½ tsp dried thyme
1 tsp cumin
½ tsp paprika
3 cloves garlic, chopped
2 tbsp stone-ground mustard
½ cup chicken broth
¼ cup honey
Salt and pepper just before serving

COOKING INSTRUCTIONS

- Melt the coconut oil in a heavy-bottomed pan over medium heat.
- Coat chicken with thyme, cumin and paprika before browning. Brown the chicken in batches, about 5 minutes a batch, and transfer to the slow cooker.
- Add the rest of the ingredients to the slow cooker, making sure the mustard and honey are mixed in, and cook on low for 6 hours.
- Salt and pepper to taste, then serve.

SERVINGS: 4

LEMON **CHICKEN SOUP**

Like many people's moms, my mom always made chicken soup when I was sick. I rarely get sick ever since I went Paleo (honestly!), but we still like to have chicken soup in winter after an exhausting day at work. Plus, homemade broth is a great source of nutrients that give you strength.

INGREDIENTS

2 tbsp ghee
1 onion, chopped
2 carrots, sliced
2 ribs celery, chopped
3 cloves garlic, crushed
3-4 lbs chicken pieces with bone and skin
2 quarts chicken broth
¼ cup lemon juice or juice from 2-3 lemons
½ bunch parsley, tied together
½ tsp fresh ground pepper
2 bay leaves
Salt and pepper just before serving

COOKING INSTRUCTIONS

- In a heavy-bottomed pan set over medium heat, melt 1 tablespoon ghee and sauté the onion, carrots and celery for 5 minutes, until the onion is translucent.
- Add the garlic, cook another 3 minutes, and transfer the mixture to the slow cooker.
- Melt the remaining ghee in the pan and brown the chicken, starting skin side down, in batches, about 5 minutes a batch, and transfer to the slow cooker.
- Add all remaining ingredients to the slow cooker and stir to combine.
- Cook on low for 6 hours.
- Remove the chicken, let it cool, then carefully remove and discard the bones and skin.
- Chop the chicken and return it to the slow cooker for 1 hour.
- Salt and pepper to taste, then serve.

SERVINGS: 6-8

SLOW-COOKER CHICKEN PESTO WITH MACADAMIA NUTS

The readers of my blog loved this dish so much that I had to include it in the book. (I repeated only a handful of my favorites.) Macadamias are a great option when nuts are called for because they have a very low Omega-6 content compared to their counterparts. They are also a healthy source of magnesium, manganese, thiamine, copper and iron. I make the sauce and brown the chicken at night. Then in the morning all I have to do is take it out of the fridge, put it in the slow cooker and hit "start."

INGREDIENTS

PESTO

1 cup fresh flat-leaf parsley leaves
2 cups fresh basil leaves
4 cloves garlic
½ cup olive oil
¼ cup macadamia nuts
2 tbsp fresh lemon juice
2 tsp fresh oregano leaves
¼ tsp sea salt
¼ tsp pepper

1 tbsp ghee
2 lbs skinless chicken thighs
¼ tsp sea salt to be added just before the end of cooking

COOKING INSTRUCTIONS

› To make the pesto, combine all the ingredients (except the chicken and ghee, of course) in a food processor and blend.

› Melt the ghee in a heavy-bottomed pan over medium heat and brown the chicken on all sides for about 5 minutes. If you are cooking for immediate use, transfer the chicken to the slow cooker and pour the pesto over it.

› If you are cooking for later use, transfer the chicken to a bowl, pour pesto over it, cover and refrigerate. When you are ready, place in the slow cooker.

› Cook on low for 5½ hours.

› Sprinkle the additional sea salt over the chicken and cook for another 30 minutes, then serve.

› For extra flavor, before pouring the sauce over the chicken, I often reduce any excess sauce in the stovetop pan over medium-low heat for 5-10 minutes.

SERVINGS: 4

CLASSIC CHICKEN CACCIATORE SLOW-COOKER STYLE

I like the traditional Italian flavors of this dish and don't miss the pasta. It's just great on its own.

INGREDIENTS

3 tbsp butter
2 lbs boneless chicken breasts or thighs
1 onion, chopped
1 bell pepper, chopped
2 stalks celery, chopped
½ lb mushrooms, sliced
4 cloves garlic, crushed
8 tomatoes, peeled and chopped
1 tsp paprika
⅛ tsp each dried basil, oregano, rosemary, thyme and marjoram
Salt and pepper just before serving

COOKING INSTRUCTIONS

› Heat a heavy-bottomed pan over medium heat and melt 1 tablespoon of butter.

› Brown the chicken in batches, about 5 minutes a batch, and transfer to the slow cooker.

› Melt the remaining butter in the pan and sauté the onion, bell pepper, celery and mushrooms for 5 minutes, until the onion is translucent.

› Add the garlic, cook for another 3 minutes, and transfer the mixture to the slow cooker.

› Add the tomatoes, paprika and herbs to the slow cooker and cook on low for 6 hours.

› Salt and pepper to taste, then serve.

SERVINGS: 4-6

CHICKEN IN RED SAUCE

My family loves peppers, especially my mom. She isn't afraid of any amount of spice! My husband loves spicy too, he adds jalapeños to everything. Pretty much any dish heavy on the peppers like this one is a hit at our house. Note that New Mexico chiles have some kick. For a milder yet similar flavor, try dried Anaheim chiles.

INGREDIENTS

6-8 chicken thighs
1 tsp salt
½ tsp ground pepper
1 tsp cumin
½ tsp smoked paprika
1 tsp oregano
1 tsp basil
2 tbsp ghee
1 onion, sliced
4 cloves garlic, sliced
8 dried red New Mexico chiles, stemmed, seeded and chopped
1 cup chicken broth
1 bay leaf
2 tomatoes, blanched, seeded and chopped
1 tbsp tomato paste
Salt and pepper just before serving

COOKING INSTRUCTIONS

› Rub the chicken with salt, pepper, cumin, paprika, oregano and basil.

› Brown the chicken on both sides in 1 tablespoon of ghee in a heavy-bottomed pan over medium heat for about 5 minutes, then transfer to the slow cooker.

› Sauté the onion in the remaining ghee until translucent.

› Add the garlic, cook another 3 minutes, until fragrant, then transfer the mixture to the slow cooker.

› Add chiles, broth, bay leaf, tomatoes and tomato paste to slow cooker. Stir to combine.

› Cook on low for 4-6 hours.

› Salt and pepper to taste, then serve.

SERVINGS: 6-8

PERSIAN CHICKEN WITH POMEGRANATE & WALNUT (FESENJAN)

This is by far my most favorite Persian dish! We make it just a few times a year. It is very rich and uses large amounts of walnuts, which have a high Omega-6 content. As delicious as this dish is, due to the strong flavor, it is difficult to eat a large portion of it so my mom usually served it for a dinner party, along with a few other main dishes because this is a dish that people either love or hate. Of course, I highly recommend it. This dish is great with cauliflower rice.

INGREDIENTS

3½ lbs bone-in, skinless chicken thighs, breasts and legs
1 tsp sea salt
4 tbsp ghee
1 large onion, thinly sliced
½ tsp cardamom
¼ tsp cinnamon
3 cloves garlic, chopped
2½ cups water
4 cups walnuts, coarsely ground
2 cups pomegranate juice
1 tbsp honey
¼ tsp ground saffron
Salt and pepper just before serving
Fresh pomegranate seeds for garnish

COOKING INSTRUCTIONS

› Pat the chicken with the salt.

› In a large heavy-bottomed pan, heat 1 tablespoon of ghee over medium heat. Brown the chicken on all sides in batches, about 5 minutes a batch, and set aside.

› Melt the remaining ghee in the pan and sauté the onion until translucent, about 5 minutes.

› Add the cardamom, cinnamon and garlic, and cook another 3 minutes.

› Add the water, bring to a boil and simmer for 8-10 minutes on low heat.

› Add the ground walnuts to the pan, forming a thick paste.

› Mix in the chicken, add pomegranate juice and honey and mix well.

› Place mixture from pan and saffron in the slow cooker.

› Cook on low for 4 hours. Remove chicken, debone, shred with 2 forks and place back in slow cooker on high with lid removed. Cook for 30 minutes to thicken the sauce.

› Salt and pepper to taste, then serve.

SERVINGS: 6

PALEO **CHICKEN VERDE**

This was one of the first meat dishes I made when I stopped being a vegetarian which had lasted through my teen and college years. Back then, I was a cooking rookie when it came to meat, so if I wasn't able to mess this one up then no one will!

This is really tasty and a go-to recipe if we have friends over for a casual dinner. For guests I usually put out some organic corn tortillas as well as lettuce so guests can choose if they are going to do a Paleo chicken-verde salad or a more traditional taco.

INGREDIENTS

½ lb tomatillos, husked and rinsed
1 serrano chili pepper
1 large poblano pepper
½ onion, chopped
¼ cup firmly packed cilantro leaves
2 cloves garlic, crushed
½ tsp cumin
2 tbsp fresh lime juice
4-6 chicken breasts
Salt and pepper just before serving
2 avocados, chopped

COOKING INSTRUCTIONS

- Place oven rack in top position and turn on the broiler. Line a baking sheet with foil and place tomatillos and peppers on it.
- Broil tomatillos and peppers until charred, about 5-6 minutes a side.
- Let stand for a few minutes until the blackened skins loosen, then pull them off (it's okay if a few pieces stay on).
- Chop the tomatillos, peppers, onion, and cilantro and add to the slow cooker with the garlic, cumin and lime juice. Stir to combine into the salsa verde (green sauce).
- Place chicken breasts in the slow cooker, pour salsa over them and cook on low for 5½ hours.
- Use 2 forks to shred the chicken, then cook for another 30 minutes.
- Salt and pepper to taste, then serve with avocado.

SERVINGS: 4-6

CAMBODIAN **CHICKEN**

Southeast Asia is a part of the world that I have not yet had a chance to visit, but it is at the top of my list of destinations. This dish is certainly one of the attractions.

INGREDIENTS

1 tbsp coconut oil
3 lbs bone-in skinless chicken thighs
3 cloves garlic, crushed
1 tbsp grated fresh ginger
3 tbsp fish sauce
3 tbsp lime juice
½ cup chicken broth
¼ cup coconut aminos
Salt and pepper just before serving

COOKING INSTRUCTIONS

› Melt the coconut oil in a heavy-bottomed pan over medium heat. Brown the chicken on all sides in batches, about 5 minutes a batch, and transfer to the slow cooker.

› Add all the other ingredients to the slow cooker, stir to combine, and cook on low for 6 hours.

› Salt and pepper to taste, then serve.

SERVINGS: 6

CHICKEN MOLE

I love a good chicken mole. The best one I have ever had was at a tiny restaurant in Santa Cruz. I've never been able to break their code, so I've created a tasty alternative. Prepare to be in the kitchen for a while though; it takes lots of chopping and measuring

INGREDIENTS

4 tbsp coconut oil
1 tbsp guajillo chili powder
¼ tsp ground black pepper
1 tsp cumin
1 tsp coriander
½ tsp anise seeds
½ tsp cinnamon
⅛ tsp nutmeg
¼ tsp ground cloves
1 tsp oregano
1 small onion, chopped
3 cloves garlic, crushed
5-6 tomatoes, peeled and diced
3 poblano chili peppers, stemmed, seeded and chopped
2 dried New Mexico chiles, stemmed, seeded and chopped
1 dried chipotle chile, stemmed, seeded and chopped
2 tomatillos, husked, rinsed and chopped
2 cups chicken broth
2 tbsp almond butter
3 tbsp cacao powder
¼ cup honey
4-6 chicken breasts
Lime and cilantro, chopped for garnish

COOKING INSTRUCTIONS

› Heat 3 tablespoons of coconut oil in a heavy-bottomed pan over medium heat. Add all the dried spices except the chiles and cacao and stir for 3 minutes.

› Add the onion and sauté until translucent, about 5 minutes.

› Add garlic and cook for another 3 minutes.

› Add the diced tomatoes, peppers, tomatillos, chicken broth, almond butter, cacao and honey and simmer for 8-10 minutes.

› Allow mixture to cool, then puree in a food processor until smooth and reserve.

› Brown the chicken in the remaining coconut oil in a heavy-bottomed pan over medium heat until browned on both sides, about 5 minutes, then transfer to the slow cooker.

› Pour reserved sauce over the chicken and cook on low for 5 hours.

› Use 2 forks to shred the chicken, then cook for another hour.

› If there is too much liquid, use a strainer to drain the chicken before serving.

SERVINGS: 6

PALEO **CHICKEN ADOBO**

My best friend gave me this recipe. Her husband is from the Philippines and this is practically their national dish. It's also one of my friend's favorite things to eat. It is easy to make and full of tart, savory and garlicky flavor. It's best to marinate the chicken overnight.

INGREDIENTS

½ cup white vinegar
½ cup coconut aminos or Tamari
½ cup water
6 cloves garlic, crushed
1 tsp black peppercorns
2 bay leaves
4 skinless chicken thighs
4 skinless chicken legs
1 tbsp ghee
Salt and pepper just before serving

COOKING INSTRUCTIONS

› Combine all ingredients except chicken and ghee in a bowl. Place the chicken in the bowl, coat with marinade, then cover and refrigerate for at least 2 hours, or even better, overnight.

› Place the sauce in the slow cooker.

› Melt the ghee in a heavy-bottomed pan over medium heat. Brown the chicken on all sides in two batches, about 5 minutes a batch, and transfer to the slow cooker.

› Cook on low for 6 hours.

› Salt and pepper to taste, then serve, spooning the sauce over the chicken.

SERVINGS: 6-8

THAI BASIL **CHICKEN**

This is my favorite Thai dish. Going out for Thai food can be difficult for Paleo dieters because the food is often sautéed in vegetable oils and the soy sauce is not gluten-free. When I went Paleo, I had to find different options. Then I figured out how to make my favorite dish at home!

INGREDIENTS

2 lbs boneless chicken thighs or breasts, cut into cubes

3 Thai red chilies (preferably fresh, but dried is okay too), chopped

2 tbsp fish sauce

1 red bell pepper, sliced

1 tbsp fresh lime juice

¼ cup coconut aminos or Tamari

1 tbsp coconut vinegar

1 tbsp grated fresh ginger

½ cup firmly packed Asian basil leaves, coarsely chopped

Salt and pepper just before serving

COOKING INSTRUCTIONS

› Add all the ingredients except the basil to the slow cooker and cook on low for 5½ hours.

› Add the basil and cook another 30 minutes.

› Salt and pepper to taste, then serve.

SERVINGS: 4

THAI CHICKEN SOUP (TOM KA GAI)

I love this chicken soup because it encompasses every aspect of Thai flavor: spicy, sweet, salty and even sour. My husband and I have had several great memories of going out for a pot of Tom Ka Gai on rainy winter nights so making this at home reminds me of good times out.

INGREDIENTS

3 skinless chicken breasts, cubed
3 cloves garlic, sliced
1 can coconut milk or 2 cups homemade coconut milk
5 cups chicken broth
1 red bell pepper, sliced
1 stalk lemongrass, finely chopped
1 cup mushrooms, sliced
1 tbsp grated fresh ginger
2 Thai peppers, chopped
2 tbsp fresh lime juice
2 tbsp fish sauce
Salt and pepper just before serving
Cilantro, chopped for garnish

COOKING INSTRUCTIONS

› Place all the ingredients in the slow cooker.

› Cook on low for 5-6 hours.

› Salt and pepper to taste, garnish with cilantro, then serve.

SERVINGS: 6

GREEN **CURRIED CHICKEN**

I am a huge fan of curries of all colors! This green curry uses Thai green chilies and is packed with flavor.

INGREDIENTS

1 small onion, sliced
4 cloves garlic, minced
2 lbs chicken breasts, cut into 1-inch cubes
2 tbsp coconut oil
1 cup coconut milk
3 tbsp green curry paste
2 kaffir lime leaves, chopped
2 tbsp fish sauce
1 red bell pepper, sliced
Salt and pepper just before serving
Fresh Asian basil leaves for garnish

COOKING INSTRUCTIONS

› Sauté the onion, garlic and chicken in coconut oil in a heavy-bottomed pan over medium heat for 8 minutes, then transfer to slow cooker.

› Place all the ingredients in the slow cooker.

› Cook on low for 6 hours.

› Salt and pepper to taste, garnish with basil leaves, then serve.

SERVINGS: 4

CAULIFLOWER **CHICKEN CURRY**

I love cauliflower and grew up eating it in many ways. It is used in a number of Persian stews, as well as served as part of a "torshi," a Persian dish of pickled vegetables. It lends itself well to Asian flavors too! This dish has it all: sweet, spicy and zesty!

INGREDIENTS

1 tsp cumin
1 tsp coriander
1 pinch of ground cloves
½ tsp turmeric
¼ tsp cayenne
2 lbs chicken breasts, cubed
2 tbsp ghee
1 onion, diced
3 cloves garlic, crushed
2 sweet potatoes, peeled and cubed
1 cauliflower, cut into florets
1 green chile, minced
1 can coconut milk or 2 cups homemade coconut milk
1 tbsp grated fresh ginger
Salt and pepper just before serving

COOKING INSTRUCTIONS

› Combine the dry spices and toss with the chicken to coat it.

› Melt 1 tablespoon of ghee in a heavy-bottomed pan over medium heat. Brown the chicken in batches for about 5 minutes a batch and set aside.

› Add the remaining ghee to the pan and sauté the onion until translucent, about 5 minutes.

› Add the garlic and cook another 3 minutes, then transfer to the slow cooker.

› Add the sweet potatoes and then cauliflower to the slow cooker. Place the chicken on top.

› Add the rest of the ingredients and cook on low for 6 hours.

› Salt and pepper to taste, then serve.

SERVINGS: 4

HAINANESE CHICKEN WITH CAULIFLOWER RICE

When I first decided to do a cookbook, I was brainstorming recipe ideas with one of my closest friends. This was the first dish she suggested. It is traditionally done on the stove top, but was easy to convert to the slow cooker. The flavors do not come from the chicken, but rather from the strong flavors of garlic and ginger in the rice and chili sauce. One of the benefits is that you end up making a meal, as well as chicken stock, all at once! By the way, this friend and her husband agreed to try the Paleo diet for 30 days and are now full converts to Paleo for several years.

INGREDIENTS

1 whole chicken, 2-3 lbs
6 slices fresh ginger, each ¼ inch thick
1 bunch scallions, cut into 1-inch pieces
2 cloves garlic, crushed
1 serrano chili pepper, chopped
1 tbsp coconut aminos or Tamari
Enough water to cover the chicken
2 tbsp coconut vinegar
1 tsp salt
½ tsp peppercorns
Fresh cilantro for garnish

COOKING INSTRUCTIONS

› Wash the chicken, remove skin and giblets and set aside, then drain chicken well.

› Stuff cavity with ginger, scallions, garlic and chili pepper.

› Rub chicken with coconut aminos.

› Place the skin and giblets in the slow cooker to add additional flavor.

› Place the chicken in the slow cooker and add the water, coconut vinegar, salt, and peppercorns.

› Cook on high for 1 hour.

› Reduce heat to low and cook for 3-4 hours, until chicken is cooked through.

› Remove the chicken from slow cooker, discard the ginger, scallions, garlic and chili pepper from cavity and pat chicken dry.

› When chicken is cool enough to handle, slice into serving-size pieces.

› Put broth through strainer and save for use in Ginger Chile Dipping Sauce (opposite) and Cauliflower Rice (page 162).

› Garnish chicken with cilantro and serve with chile dipping sauce, cauliflower rice, and sliced English cucumbers.

SERVINGS: 6

GINGER CHILE **DIPPING SAUCE**

INGREDIENTS

6 chopped fresh Thai chiles
3 medium cloves garlic, minced
½ shallot, chopped
2 inches fresh ginger, chopped
1 tbsp fresh lime juice
2 tbsp hot chicken broth (from the slow cooker)
1 tbsp coconut aminos or Tamari
½ tsp salt
½ tsp honey
Salt just before serving

COOKING INSTRUCTIONS

› Blend all ingredients in a food processor.

› Add salt to taste, then serve.

SERVINGS: 4

CAULIFLOWER RICE (NOT A SLOW-COOKER RECIPE)

INGREDIENTS

1 head cauliflower, trimmed and coarsely chopped

2 tbsp butter

1 medium onion, diced

4 cloves garlic, crushed

1 tbsp grated fresh ginger

½ tsp sea salt

1 cup chicken broth (from the slow cooker)

COOKING INSTRUCTIONS

› Place the cauliflower in a food processor and blend until it is the texture of rice.

› Melt the butter in a heavy-bottomed pan over medium-high heat. Sauté the onion until soft, about 5 minutes.

› Add the garlic and ginger, and sauté until fragrant, about another 3 minutes.

› Add the cauliflower and salt, and cook for 2 minutes.

› Add broth and simmer for about 10 minutes or until all the liquid has evaporated.

SERVINGS: 4

INDIAN **GINGER CHICKEN**

The aromas of Indian food are such a delight, and this dish will fill your house with them.

INGREDIENTS

2 tbsp coconut oil
4 boneless, skinless chicken breasts
1 onion, chopped
2 cloves garlic, crushed
3 Anaheim peppers, chopped
Juice of 1 lemon
1 tsp cardamom
1 tsp coriander
½ tsp turmeric
½ tsp paprika
3 cloves
1 stick of cinnamon
4 inches of fresh ginger, chopped
1 bay leaf
2 tomatoes, chopped
1 cup coconut milk
Salt and pepper just before serving

COOKING INSTRUCTIONS

- Melt 1 tablespoon of coconut oil in a heavy-bottomed pan over medium heat. Brown the chicken on both sides, about 5 minutes, and transfer to the slow cooker.
- Sauté the onion in the remaining oil until translucent, about 5 minutes.
- Add the garlic and peppers, cook another 3 minutes and transfer the mixture to the slow cooker.
- Add the rest of the ingredients and cook on low for 6 hours.
- Salt and pepper to taste, then serve.

SERVINGS: 4-6

MULLIGATAWNY

I have founds foods from many parts of the world to be made primarily of whole ingredients and full of flavor. This Indian stew is one of those dishes. It's a little different from the standard curry so offers a great new taste.

INGREDIENTS

2 lbs boneless, skinless chicken thighs
½ tsp cinnamon
¼ tsp ground cloves
1 tsp ground coriander
1 tsp cumin
½ tsp turmeric
2 tbsp coconut oil
1 onion, chopped
4 cloves garlic, minced
1 carrot, chopped
2 green chili peppers, minced
1 tbsp grated fresh ginger
1 apple, peeled, cored and chopped
1 tbsp lemon juice
4 cups chicken broth
Salt and pepper just before serving

COOKING INSTRUCTIONS

› Toss the chicken thighs in the combined dried spices.

› Melt 1 tablespoon of the coconut oil in a heavy-bottomed pan over medium heat. Brown the chicken on all sides, about 5 minutes, and transfer to the slow cooker.

› Add the remaining coconut oil to the pan and sauté the onion until translucent, about 5 minutes.

› Add the garlic, carrot and chili peppers, cook until fragrant, about 3 minutes, and transfer the mixture to the slow cooker.

› Add the rest of the ingredients to the slow cooker and cook on low for 6 hours.

› Salt and pepper to taste, then serve.

SERVINGS: 4-6

CORNISH HENS WITH MUSTARD SAUCE

Mustard gives this dish a tangy zip to complement the classic aroma of rosemary.

INGREDIENTS

1 tbsp butter
2 Cornish hens
Juice of 1 lemon
½ cup chicken stock
1 tbsp chopped fresh rosemary
1 tsp dried thyme
2 cloves garlic, crushed
3 tbsp stone-ground mustard
Salt and pepper just before serving

COOKING INSTRUCTIONS

- Melt the butter in a heavy-bottomed pan over medium heat.
- Brown the hens about 5 minutes, handling them carefully to avoid tearing the skin, and transfer to the slow cooker.
- Pour the lemon juice and stock over the meat.
- Sprinkle the rosemary and thyme over the meat and sauce, add the garlic and cook on low for 6 hours.
- Remove the hens and place the leftover liquid in a sauce pan.
- Stir in the mustard, reduce for about 5 minutes over medium heat and pour over the hens before serving.
- Salt and pepper to taste, then serve.

SERVINGS: 2

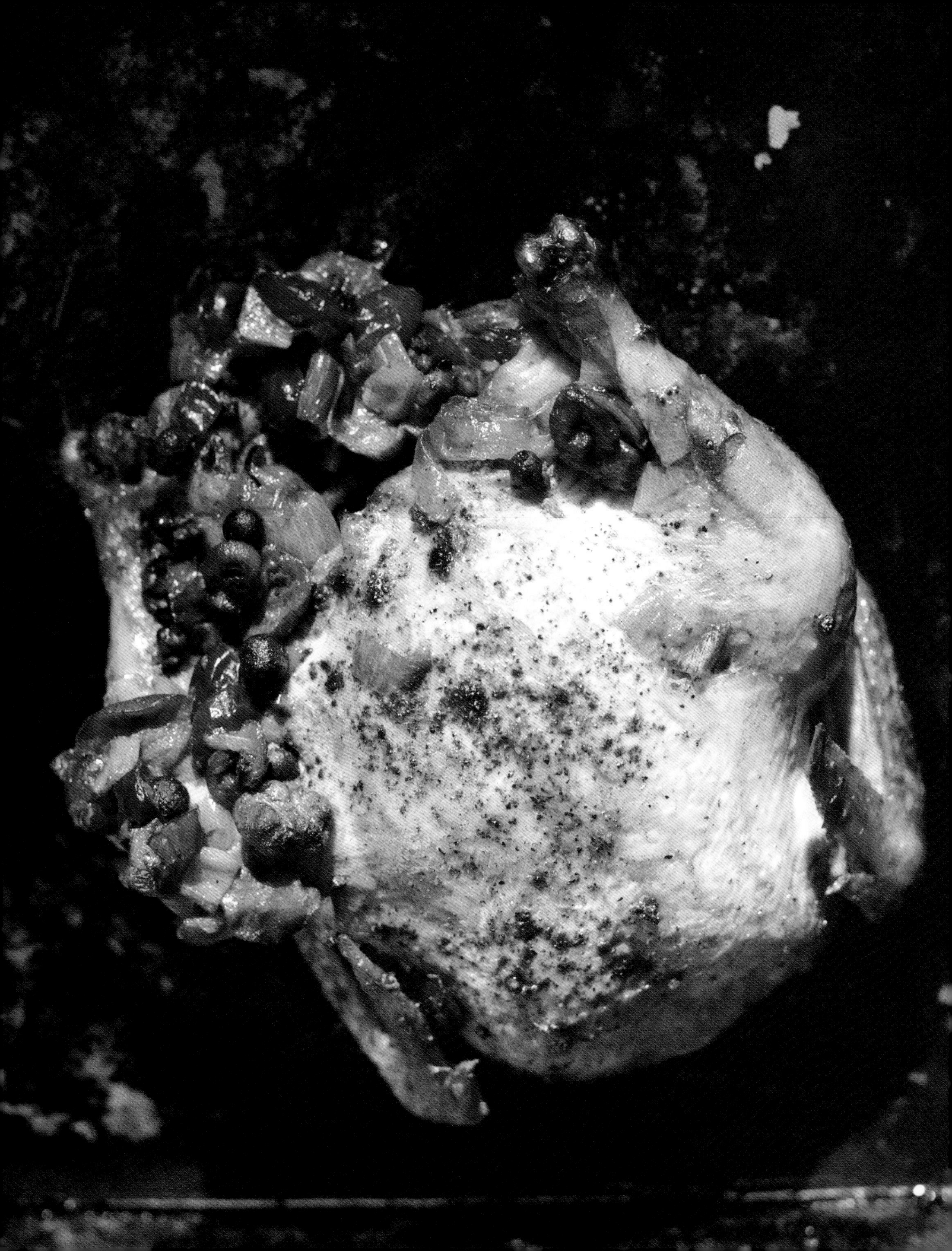

CORNISH HENS WITH WALNUTS AND DRIED CRANBERRIES

This is a great and festive dish for a special dinner for two. It's like the fall season wrapped up in one dish.

INGREDIENTS

2 tbsp coconut oil
2 Cornish hens
4 shallots, chopped
¼ cup chopped walnuts
¼ cup dried cranberries
½ tsp cardamom
½ tsp cinnamon
¼ tsp nutmeg
½ tsp allspice
Juice of 1 lemon
½ cup chicken broth or white wine
Salt and pepper just before serving

COOKING INSTRUCTIONS

- Heat 1 tablespoon coconut oil in a heavy-bottomed pan over medium heat.
- Brown each hen about 5 minutes, handling them carefully to avoid tearing the skin, then transfer to the slow cooker.
- Add the remaining coconut oil to the pan and sauté the shallots for 5 minutes, until translucent.
- Add the nuts, berries and spices, and cook for 2 minutes, until the fruit is softened. Add mixture to the slow cooker, around the meat.
- Add the lemon juice and white wine or broth, and cook on low for 6 hours.
- Salt and pepper to taste, then serve.

SERVINGS: 2

TURKEY IN CRANBERRY AND GINGER SAUCE

This is perfect to make around the holidays, especially if you are planning a Thanksgiving dinner for only a few guests! The ginger brightens up the flavor of the traditional cranberry sauce.

INGREDIENTS

2 large skinless turkey breasts, cut into 2 chunks
1 tbsp ghee
1 lb cranberries
2 pears, peeled and sliced
1 tbsp grated ginger
¼ cup water
½ cup honey
Salt and pepper just before serving

COOKING INSTRUCTIONS

› Brown the turkey breasts in the ghee in a heavy-bottomed pan over medium heat, about 5 minutes, and transfer to the slow cooker.

› Add all the remaining ingredients to a saucepan and bring to a boil, stirring occasionally.

› Reduce heat to medium, and cook uncovered until most of the cranberries pop and the pears are tender.

› Using a wooden spoon, crush the pears to create a more sauce-like consistency.

› Pour cranberry sauce over the turkey and cook on low for 4-6 hours.

› Salt and pepper to taste, then serve.

SERVINGS: 4

TURKEY CHILI

Paleo chili always reminds me of when I first started following the Paleo diet. It was one of the first dishes I made. I remember thinking if Paleo eating tastes this good, then this diet change will be no problem. It proved to be right!

INGREDIENTS

2 tbsp ghee
1 onion, chopped
1 green pepper, chopped
2 Anaheim chili peppers, chopped
1½ lbs ground turkey
2 tbsp chili powder
1 tsp coriander
½ tsp cumin
1 tsp dried oregano
½ tsp chili pepper flakes
¼ tsp cayenne pepper
½ tsp paprika
2 tbsp tomato paste
1 jalapeño pepper, chopped
2 cups chopped tomatoes
2 cups beef broth
Salt and pepper just before serving

COOKING INSTRUCTIONS

› Melt 1 tablespoon of ghee in a heavy-bottomed pan over medium heat. Sauté the onion, green pepper and Anaheim peppers about 5 minutes, until onion is translucent.

› Add the ground turkey, chili powder, coriander, cumin, oregano, pepper flakes, cayenne, paprika and tomato paste. Cook until the turkey is browned, about 8 minutes, and transfer to the slow cooker.

› Add the jalapeño, tomatoes and beef broth to the slow cooker, and cook on low for 6 hours.

› Salt and pepper to taste, then serve.

SERVINGS: 6

chapter six

DELICIOUSLY DONE **DUCK**

I AM PRETTY NEW TO DUCK MYSELF. I just started eating it a couple of years ago. I had it for the first time when eating Thai food and instantly fell in love. Now I order it every chance I get. Like most other farmed animals, most ducks are given feed, so look for free-range ducks raised on pasture with a varied diet. Duck is a great source of protein, vitamins and minerals. And duck fat is great to cook with!

SHREDDED ROASTED DUCK FOR BREAKFAST OR LUNCH

One of the first times I ever had duck, was with two of my closest girlfriends in San Diego. We were at a terrific little restaurant in Encinitas. They served the duck very simply with lots of fresh thyme and a side of eggs for breakfast which was fantastic. In this recipe, the moist, rich flavor of the duck really stands on its own.

INGREDIENTS

- **1 duck, quartered and skinned (save skin to render cooking fat for another dish)**
- **2 tbsp ghee**
- **½ onion, sliced**
- **¼ cup chicken broth**
- **5 sprigs of fresh thyme, minced, plus 2 additional sprigs**
- **Salt and pepper just before serving**
- **Boston lettuce leaves for serving**

COOKING INSTRUCTIONS

- Lightly coat the duck with a thin layer of ghee (1 tablespoon), then brown the duck in the broiler, skin side up, for 5 minutes, turning once and watching carefully so it doesn't burn. Then transfer to the slow cooker.
- Sauté onion in the remaining ghee in a heavy-bottomed pan over medium heat for 5 minutes, until translucent, and place in the slow cooker.
- Add the broth and minced thyme, and cook on low for 7-8 hours.
- Shred the duck with 2 forks and add additional thyme.
- Salt and pepper to taste, then serve on Boston lettuce leaves or with eggs for breakfast!

SERVINGS: 4

DUCK WITH BERRY PIQUANT SAUCE

This is another elegant dish, perfect for festivities or guests. The rich flavor of duck can hold its own again strong sweet tastes which makes the duck dishes a little more fun and interesting.

INGREDIENTS

4 duck breasts
1 tbsp butter
4 shallots, finely chopped
2 cloves garlic, crushed
¼ cup red wine
¼ cup apple cider vinegar
½ cup chicken stock
2 tsp tomato paste
1 tsp stone-ground mustard
2 sprigs of tarragon leaves, chopped
1 sprig of rosemary leaves, chopped
2 cups red currants
Salt and pepper just before serving

COOKING INSTRUCTIONS

› In a heavy-bottomed pan over medium heat, brown the breasts, skin side down, in the butter, about 5 minutes. Transfer to the slow cooker, placing them skin side up.

› Use the remaining fat in the pan to sauté the shallots for 5 minutes, until translucent.

› Add the garlic and cook another 3 minutes, until fragrant, then transfer the mixture to the slow cooker.

› In a separate bowl, combine the wine, vinegar, stock, tomato paste, mustard, herbs and berries and stir until the mustard and tomato paste are incorporated. Then pour over duck breasts in the slow cooker.

› Cook on low for 6-8 hours.

› Place extra liquid in a sauce pan over medium-low heat, reduce for 5 minutes and pour over the duck.

› Salt and pepper to taste, then serve.

SERVINGS: 4

ROAST DUCK WITH PEARS

This dish just shouts holiday season to me. I love to cook food that takes our families out of their comfort zones during that time of the year. I am not a huge fan of turkey; I would consider making this instead sometime!

INGREDIENTS

2 tbsp ghee
4 duck breasts
1 onion, sliced
2 pears, sliced
¼ cup dried cranberries
½ cup white wine
¼ tsp cinnamon
Salt and pepper just before serving

COOKING INSTRUCTIONS

- Melt 1 tablespoon of ghee in a heavy-bottomed pan over medium heat. Brown the duck skin side down for 5 minutes and transfer to the slow cooker, placing them skin side up.
- Add the remaining ghee to the pan and sauté the onion for 5 minutes, until translucent.
- Add the pears and cranberries to the pan, cook another 3 minutes, and transfer the mixture to the slow cooker, being careful not to break the pear slices.
- Add the white wine to the slow cooker and sprinkle the cinnamon over the breasts and sauce.
- Cook on low for 6-8 hours.
- Salt and pepper to taste, then serve.

SERVINGS: 4

DUCK LEGS WITH YAMS

This simple and delicious one-pot meal will impress your friends. The sweetness of the yams complements the savoriness of the duck. The wine gives it a nice rich finish.

INGREDIENTS

8 duck legs
1 tbsp ghee
3-4 yams, peeled and cubed
3 sprigs of thyme
2 cloves garlic, crushed
3 shallots, chopped
½ cup chicken stock
½ cup Marsala wine
2 bay leaves
¼ tsp allspice
Salt and pepper just before serving

COOKING INSTRUCTIONS

- Lightly coat the duck legs with ghee and broil skin side up for 5 minutes, watching carefully so the skin doesn't burn.
- Place the yams at the bottom of the slow cooker and add the rest of the ingredients.
- Place the duck on top of the yams and cook on low for 6-8 hours.
- Salt and pepper to taste, then serve.

SERVINGS: 4

SPICY **DUCK CURRY**

I think we don't eat enough duck in America. I used to just stick to the typical meats too, pretty much beef and chicken. The restrictions of the Paleo diet expanded my horizons in a good way. Now I jump at opportunities to try real foods that are out of the ordinary, and duck has become one of my favorites, especially in curry. And this one is a really easy one to make.

INGREDIENTS

4 whole boneless duck breasts, skin removed, cut into large chunks (save skin to render cooking fat for a different dish)

1 tbsp Thai red curry paste (the instant stuff that you don't have to cook)

¼ tsp cayenne pepper

1 stalk lemongrass, finely chopped

1 tbsp grated fresh ginger

½ tsp cumin

½ tsp coriander

1 tbsp fish sauce

1 red pepper, chopped

1 red onion, sliced

2 tomatoes, peeled and chopped

1 cup coconut milk

1 bunch fresh basil leaves, chopped and added just before serving

Salt and pepper just before serving

COOKING INSTRUCTIONS

› Add all the ingredients except the fresh basil to the slow cooker.

› Stir to make sure the curry paste is incorporated.

› Cook on low for 6-8 hours.

› Add the basil, salt and pepper to taste, then serve.

SERVINGS: 4-6

ABOUT INTERMITTENT FASTING

Intermittent fasting is an eating style that alternates between periods of fasting and eating. The fasting is typically longer than the overnight fast we normally do and most often ranges from 12 to 48 hours.

Fasting has been shown to be beneficial in several areas including weight/fat loss, blood lipid and inflammation management, neurological health, appetite and blood sugar control, fighting cancer and may increase overall life span. With all of the pros it may seem that intermittent fasting is the way to go for everyone. This is not necessarily the case and in some situations it may do more harm than good. It is not recommended that one begin fasting unless he/she has all the other details in place. This means clean eating, a smart exercise program, adequate sleep and minimal life stress. If any of these things are out of line, fasting will put you on the "fast" path to adrenal fatigue and further potential problems. Other situations where fasting may be contraindicated include pregnancy, issues with blood-sugar regulation (diabetes), in small children, and those under a great deal of stress as rigorous training program.

Then who is it good for? If you've got your diet, exercise, sleep and stress well managed and are looking for something to experiment with, then give it a go. Just be smart!

THERE ARE SEVERAL METHODS OF FASTING, WITH THE MOST COMMON PROTOCOLS BEING:

Meal Skipping: This is simply "missing a meal"—whether it be because you aren't hungry or it's not convenient—say, if you are traveling.

Condensed-Eating Windows: Eating time is limited to a specified number of hours based on schedule and/or preference. The window is usually somewhere between four and seven hours.

24-48 Hour Fast: This is exactly as it sounds, 24-48 hours of no eating followed by resumed normal eating patterns.

Every Other Day Fast: This is usually done for a week or longer and involves alternating between a 24-hour fast followed by a day of eating for a specified period of time.

Personal Protocols: This can also be set up to fit individual needs, goals, and responses. You might fast on Tuesdays and Fridays because of your work schedule, for example. These protocols are tailored to fit what works for your given situation.

chapter seven

FANTASTIC FISH AND SEAFOOD FOR ANCIENT MARINERS

INCLUDING WILD-CAUGHT FISH IN OUR DIETS is a great way to increase our omega-3 fatty-acid intake. Omega-3s are what are called essential fatty acids; the body doesn't make them so we have to get them from the food we eat. Fish obtain Omega-3s from algae or plankton in their diets. Like other feedlot animals, farmed fish are not given a proper diet, are often treated with antibiotics or given feed that has been treated with pesticides, so are low in Omega-3s. The best sources of Omega-3 fatty acids are oily, cold-water fish, such as salmon, herring, mackerel, anchovies and sardines.

Fish can be cooked in a slow cooker, but fish requires much less cooking time than other proteins. Shellfish is harder. We didn't include too many recipes because the slow cooker often doesn't make cooking seafood more convenient or easy.

LEMON TARRAGON **TILAPIA**

This is a great garlicky and buttery fish dish that's easy to make. The dish contains a lot of butter, and if you are sensitive to dairy foods, I would skip this one.

INGREDIENTS

2 sticks of butter
6 cloves garlic, crushed
½ cup fresh lemon juice
1 tsp lemon zest
2 lbs tilapia fillets
3 sprigs of fresh tarragon, chopped
Salt and pepper just before serving

COOKING INSTRUCTIONS

› Place the butter, garlic, lemon juice and zest in the slow cooker and cook on low for 4 hours.

› Add the tilapia and tarragon, and cook for another 40 minutes, until the fish is opaque and cooked through.

› Salt and pepper to taste, then serve.

SERVINGS: 4-6

SLOW-COOKED **SALMON**

I eat salmon more than any other fish. I have to admit it's not my favorite fish, but it's so healthy that I buy it often. It's considered by many nutritionists, both Paleo and not, to be a superfood and a great source of Omega-3 fatty acids as well as Vitamin D, which is not found in many foods. It's important to get wild-caught salmon because farmed fish provide less Omega-3s. You can see the difference in the deeper red color of the wild-caught fish. In this dish, the salmon is essentially poached in the slow cooker and white wine.

INGREDIENTS

2 lbs salmon fillets, cut across the fish into 4 pieces
2 cloves garlic, crushed
½ cup white wine
2 tbsp fresh lemon juice
1 tsp lemon zest
4 shallots, sliced
2 tbsp macadamia nut oil
½ tsp dried rosemary
½ tsp dried thyme
Salt and pepper just before serving

COOKING INSTRUCTIONS

› Place salmon in the slow cooker skin side down.

› Add the garlic, white wine, lemon juice and zest to the slow cooker, making sure the garlic is in the liquid.

› Place the sliced shallots on top of the fillets and drizzle the oil over the top.

› Sprinkle the dried herbs over the fillets and sauce, then cook on low for 1½ to 2 hours.

› Place extra liquid in a sauce pan over medium-low heat, reduce by half, about 5 minutes, and pour over the plated salmon.

› Salt and pepper to taste, then serve.

SERVINGS: 4

SEAFOOD **BOUILLABAISSE**

Bouillabaisse is another versatile soup dish that has numerous variations all along the Mediterranean coast. I like it because I consider it an easy, throw-together delicious dish packed with herbs and flavor.

INGREDIENTS

2 tbsp ghee
2 leeks, chopped
2 carrots, sliced
1 fennel bulb, chopped
4 cloves garlic, crushed
1 tbsp tomato paste
6 tomatoes, peeled and chopped or 1 can chopped tomatoes
1 cup fish stock
1 cup dry white wine
A couple strands of saffron
1 tsp fennel seeds
¼ tsp cayenne pepper
½ lb mussels, scrubbed and debearded
½ lb sea scallops
½ lb shrimp, peeled and deveined
1 lb tilapia, cut into 1-inch cubes
Salt and pepper just before serving

COOKING INSTRUCTIONS

› Melt the ghee in a heavy-bottomed pan over medium heat and sauté the leeks, carrots and fennel for 5 minutes, until the leeks are soft.

› Add the garlic and tomato paste, and cook another 3 minutes, until garlic is fragrant.

› Add the tomatoes and simmer for 10 minutes, then transfer the mixture into the slow cooker.

› Add the stock, wine, saffron, fennel seeds and cayenne to the slow cooker and cook on low for 6-8 hours.

› Turn the slow cooker to high and add the seafood in this order: mussels—which should be under the liquid for the most part—scallops, shrimp and tilapia, which should be above the liquid.

› Cook on high for 45 minutes, until the fish is cooked through and the mussels have opened.

› Discard any unopened mussels, salt and pepper to taste, then serve.

SERVINGS: 4-6

CIOPPINO

This fun and fantastic fish stew originated in San Francisco and was made up of local fishermen's typical catch of the day. It thus goes nicely with the Paleo philosophy of cooking what is naturally available.

INGREDIENTS

1 onion, chopped
1 tbsp butter
5 cloves garlic, crushed
1 green bell pepper, chopped
2 carrots, sliced
3 tbsp tomato paste
2 cups white wine
1 cup chicken stock
8 tomatoes, peeled and chopped
2 bay leaves
½ tsp dried basil
½ tsp dried marjoram
½ tsp dried oregano
1 tsp dried thyme
1 spicy pepper, chopped
1 tsp paprika
½ lb clams, scrubbed
½ lb mussels, scrubbed and debearded
½ lb scallops
1 cup crabmeat
1 lb shrimp, peeled and deveined
1 lb cod fillets, cubed
½ cup fresh chopped parsley for garnish
Salt and pepper just before serving

COOKING INSTRUCTIONS

› Sauté the onion in the butter in a heavy-bottomed pan over medium heat for 5 minutes.

› Add the garlic, bell pepper, carrots and tomato paste to the pan, cook another 3 minutes, until the garlic is fragrant, and transfer the mixture to the slow cooker.

› Add the wine, stock, tomatoes, herbs, spicy pepper and paprika to the slow cooker, and cook on low for 6-8 hours.

› Turn the slow cooker to high and place the clams and mussels into the liquid.

› Add the scallops, crab and shrimp on top, then the fish last above the liquid.

› Cook on high for 45 minutes, until the fish is opaque and most of the clams and mussels have opened, discarding any unopened shellfish. Garnish with parsley, salt and pepper to taste, then serve.

SERVINGS: 6

JAMBALAYA

Here's my Paleo take on a jambalaya. This dish uses a lot of pepper which potentially have health benefits and come with the more obvious advantage of tasting great. It's packed with herbs and different tastes that get combined nicely in the slow cooker. In fact, this is one of the first dishes I made in my slow cooker. Even though it has a lot of ingredients, it's hard to mess up. It's still one of my favorites.

INGREDIENTS

4 slices bacon, cut into 1-inch pieces
1 tbsp ghee
1 large onion, chopped
1 large green bell pepper, chopped
1 cup chopped celery
3 cloves garlic, crushed
1 lb chicken breasts, cut into 1-inch cubes
1 lb spicy sausage like chorizo or hot Italian sausage, casing removed and crumbled
8 tomatoes, peeled and chopped, with juices
2 cups chicken broth
½ tsp dried oregano
1 tsp dried parsley
½ tsp dried thyme
2 tsp Cajun seasoning
½ tsp cayenne pepper
½ tsp paprika
1 lb cooked shrimp without tails
Salt and pepper just before serving

COOKING INSTRUCTIONS

› Heat a heavy-bottomed pan over medium heat, add bacon and cook until crisp, about 5 minutes, then reserve.

› Add ghee, onion, bell pepper and celery to the bacon grease, and cook until tender, another 5 minutes.

› Add the garlic, cook another 3 minutes and transfer the mixture to the slow cooker.

› Brown the chicken and sausage on all sides in the pan for about 5 minutes, and transfer to the slow cooker.

› Add the tomatoes, chicken broth, dried herbs and spices to the slow cooker and cook on low for 7½ hours.

› Add the shrimp and cook another 30 minutes.

› Add bacon bits, salt and pepper to taste, then serve.

SERVINGS: 12

THAI-INSPIRED COCONUT PUMPKIN SOUP

I am always looking for new things to do with pumpkin, or in this case an Asian variety called kabocha squash, in the fall season. I love the naturally sweet flavor. Pumpkin/kabocha lends itself well to Asian dishes, and is delicious with coconut milk. The refreshing flavor of the lemongrass is also a great complement.

INGREDIENTS

1 small kabocha squash or pumpkin, peeled and diced
1 yam, peeled and diced
2 small red or green chilies, sliced
3 cups coconut milk
3 cups chicken stock
1 shallot, minced
3 cloves garlic
3 stalks lemongrass, minced
½ cup basil leaves
½ tsp shrimp paste
2 tbsp fish sauce
1 lb cooked shrimp, peeled and deveined
Salt just before serving

COOKING INSTRUCTIONS

› Place all ingredients except the shrimp in the slow cooker, starting with the squash and yam.

› Cook on low for 6-8 hours, until the squash and yam are tender.

› Add the shrimp and cook another 30 minutes.

› Salt to taste, then serve.

SERVINGS: 4

SWEET AND SOUR **SHRIMP**

I love the flavors in this dish and am a sucker for a light refreshing entrée with some fruit mixed in. The coconut aminos give the dish a nice balance of salty and sweet.

INGREDIENTS

½ cup chicken or fish stock
1 cup fresh pineapple chunks
1 cup, thinly sliced onion
3 cloves garlic, crushed
2 tsp minced ginger
2 tbsp apple cider vinegar
2 tbsp coconut aminos
1 tsp red pepper flakes
1 cup chunks of green bell peppers
1 lb cooked shrimp, peeled
Salt and pepper just before serving

COOKING INSTRUCTIONS

› Place all ingredients except shrimp in the slow cooker.

› Cook on low for 4 hours.

› Add the shrimp and cook for another 30 minutes.

› Salt and pepper to taste, then serve.

SERVINGS: 4

IODINE AND THE PALEO DIET

Iodine is an important nutrient, but many Paleo-lifestyle followers do not get a great deal of it. The No. 1 dietary source of iodine for most people is table salt. Kelp and seaweed are also rich in the nutrient and trace amounts are found in many vegetables. When deficient in iodine, thyroid function is compromised, and it is many times taken in supplement form by persons with low thyroid-hormone levels.

We recommend you do not eliminate or avoid table salt. If you are eating any packaged foods like beef jerky, canned tuna, cured meats, bacon or sausage, for example, you are likely getting iodine via the salt used in these products. If a person has a low-functioning thyroid, I often suggest adding a low-dose iodine supplement, especially if they are using non-iodized salt and few processed/salty foods.

WEIGHT LOSS

Losing weight is an $88 billion industry. Surveys show that some people would give up five years of life if they could lose the weight. Losing weight is a goal that nearly everyone at one time or another has had. Weight loss, the ever-sought after dream of having six-pack abs and a perfect body is the stuff that makes news headlines, special products, drugs and surgeries designed to help get the job done. Does it really have to be this difficult? Are we so attached to fast food, soda, refined sugar and processed "food-like" substances? Sadly, the answer is yes. Fortunately, more and more people are realizing healthy food doesn't have to be "fat-free" and taste like cardboard.

A Paleo way of life is a great tool for weight loss. There is no feeling hungry, no pills, no special foods to buy and everything you need can be found at the grocery store. But how exactly does this "miracle diet" work?

The standard American diet (SAD) is largely made up of high-calorie, low-nutrient processed foods. Due to the high carbohydrate and sugar content in the SAD, insulin levels are in a constant state of elevation. Insulin is the hormone that turns on the signal for fat storage. The more sugar in our blood, the more insulin we need to take it out. Once muscle and liver glycogen stores are full, all the extra sugar in the blood is stored as fat. The Paleo style of eating eliminates processed, low-nutrient-dense, sugar and carbohydrate-laden foods and replaces them with nutrient-dense vegetables, proteins, and moderate amounts of healthy fats. There is less sugar in the blood and less insulin signaling fat storage.

Vegetables and some fruit are the primary carbohydrate sources in a Paleo diet. Compared to a plate of pasta or a sugary soda, the amount of carbohydrate in vegetables is significantly lower and the vegetables are much more nutritious! It is very difficult to eat too much broccoli; too many potato chips is a different story. The types of food consumed in the Paleo diet fill us up without filling us out.

Carbohydrates are water-holding molecules. When breads, cereals, soda, pasta and other sugary or carb-laden dishes are removed from the diet and replaced with vegetables and protein, the body loses a great deal of water. This is often the explanation for rapid weight loss in the first week after making the switch to the Paleo diet.

The foods that are part of the Paleo plan, lots of non-starchy vegetables, animal protein, moderate amounts of healthy fats and some fruit, are nutrient-dense without being calorie dense. Eliminating calorie-dense sodas, fast and processed foods, and foods high in carbohydrate results in the body using stored fat for energy instead of carbohydrates.

In addition, many people are sensitive to the food components, chemicals and artificial ingredients in today's food supply. Substances like wheat, dairy, antibiotics and pesticides all have an effect on our body's hormones. Many times these effects result in the development of autoimmune and other conditions that can have a marked effect on hormones that regulate both weight and appetite. A Paleo lifestyle minimizes exposure to foods and agents that may contribute to hormone dysfunction.

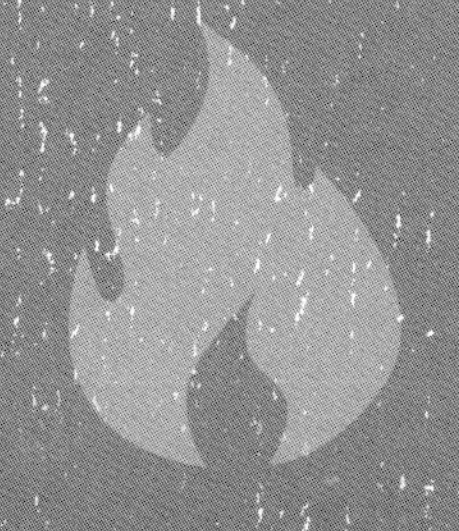

chapter eight

PALEO SENSATION SLOW-COOKED VEGGIES

VEGETABLES ARE A LARGE COMPONENT OF THE PALEO DIET. This is where we get most of our carbs. And of course they are a great source of vitamins and minerals. It's important to include a wide variety of vegetables of different colors in the diet to give your body a wide range of nutrients. If you have a difficult time digesting raw vegetables, the slow cooker is a great tool. It produces tasty, well-cooked vegetables that are easier to digest. It's best to purchase the highest-quality vegetables you can afford — organic and free of pesticides. I highly recommend joining a good CSA that will provide your household with a steady flow of fresh organic vegetables at a reasonable price.

PERSIAN **MIXED VEGETABLES**

In my parents' household, we usually have this as a side, but it is hearty enough to eat on its own if you aren't in the mood for meat.

INGREDIENTS

3 sweet potatoes, peeled and chopped 1-to 1½-inch pieces
1 onion, chopped
3 cloves garlic, minced
3 carrots, sliced
1 large eggplant, diced
4 tomatoes, chopped
1 cup chicken stock
1 tsp turmeric
Pinch of saffron
½ tsp coriander
1 tbsp tomato paste
Salt and pepper just before serving

COOKING INSTRUCTIONS

› Place the sweet potatoes at the bottom of the slow cooker and add the rest of the ingredients.

› Cook on low for 4 hours or until veggies are tender.

› Salt and pepper to taste, then serve.

SERVINGS: 4-6

RATATOUILLE

This is a traditional Italian favorite that turns out nicely in the slow cooker. It is a great main dish, but also can serve as a side.

INGREDIENTS

2 eggplants, cut into 1-inch cubes
2 onions, chopped
2 large zucchini, sliced
3 bell peppers, seeded and chopped
6 tomatoes, halved, seeded and chopped
½ tsp oregano
1 tbsp chopped fresh parsley
1 bunch of basil leaves, coarsely chopped
¼ cup olive oil
Salt and pepper just before serving

COOKING INSTRUCTIONS

› Layer the slow cooker with vegetables and herbs, starting with the eggplants and reserving the fresh basil.

› Cook on low for 4-5 hours.

› Add the basil and drizzle with olive oil. Salt and pepper to taste, then serve.

SERVINGS: 4-6

VEGETABLE **CURRY**

I really love a good curry. Cumin, coriander and turmeric are such flavorful spices. Here I have used chicken stock instead of coconut milk and added more spices to give a different flavor.

INGREDIENTS

1 onion, chopped
2 carrots, sliced
1 tbsp coconut oil
3 cloves garlic, crushed
1 lb sweet potatoes, peeled and cubed
1 head of cauliflower, cut into florets
1 tbsp grated fresh ginger
1 tbsp cumin
2 tsp coriander
½ tsp turmeric
½ tsp cinnamon
1 tsp paprika
1 cup chicken stock
Salt and pepper just before serving

COOKING INSTRUCTIONS

› In a heavy-bottomed pan over medium heat, sauté the onion and carrots in the coconut oil for about 5 minutes, until the onion is translucent.

› Add the garlic, cook another 3 minutes, until fragrant, then transfer the mixture to the slow cooker.

› Place the sweet potatoes at the bottom of the slow cooker and add the rest of the ingredients. Cook on low for 4-5 hours.

› Salt and pepper to taste, then serve.

SERVINGS: 4-6

SOUPS

PROVENÇAL VEGETABLE SOUP, PALEO STYLE

This is a nice light soup perfect for serving your garden harvest. Sometimes simple is better and this is best if you make the chicken stock from scratch.

INGREDIENTS

1 tbsp ghee
4 medium carrots, peeled and chopped
2 medium leeks, white and light green parts only, washed and sliced
2 stalks celery, chopped
4 cloves garlic, crushed
6 cups chicken stock
2 zucchini, sliced
2 summer squash, sliced
6 ripe tomatoes, peeled, seeded and chopped
3 fresh sprigs of thyme
¼ cup minced fresh basil
2 tbsp minced fresh parsley
Salt and pepper just before serving

COOKING INSTRUCTIONS

- Melt the ghee in a heavy-bottomed pan over medium heat and sauté the carrots, leeks and celery for 5 minutes, until the leeks are soft.
- Add the garlic, cook another 3 minutes, then transfer the mixture to the slow cooker.
- Add the rest of the ingredients and cook on low for 3-4 hours.
- Salt and pepper to taste, then serve.

SERVINGS: 6

YAM, LEEK AND SAUSAGE SOUP

I love using leeks in a dish like this because they are much sweeter yet milder than their counterparts in the onion family, so you can use a large amount.

INGREDIENTS

2 yams, peeled and diced
2 large leeks, white part only, sliced and well cleaned
2 stalks celery, chopped
1 tbsp butter
3 cloves garlic, crushed
½ tsp thyme
4 cups chicken broth
1 lb kielbasa sausages, sliced
Salt and pepper just before serving

COOKING INSTRUCTIONS

› Place the yams in the bottom of the slow cooker.

› In a heavy-bottomed pan, sauté the leeks and celery in the butter until the leeks are soft, about 5 minutes.

› Add the garlic, cook for another 3 minutes and transfer mixture to the slow cooker.

› Add the rest of the ingredients and cook on low for 6-8 hours.

› Salt and pepper to taste, then serve.

SERVINGS: 6

BUTTERNUT SQUASH SOUP

I love butternut squash. It is not only full of nutrients, but has a sweet and nutty flavor that is so perfect on a fall day. The coconut milk gives it a nice creamy finish.

INGREDIENTS

1 tbsp butter
1 leek, cleaned and chopped
3 cloves garlic, crushed
1 large butternut squash, peeled, seeded, and cut into cubes
5 cups chicken broth
1 cup coconut milk
½ tsp dried thyme
½ tsp dried rosemary
Salt and pepper just before serving

COOKING INSTRUCTIONS

- Heat the butter in a heavy-bottomed pan over medium heat and sauté the leek until soft, about 5 minutes.
- Add the garlic, cook another 3 minutes, until fragrant, then transfer the mixture to the slow cooker.
- Add the rest of the ingredients and cook on low for 6-8 hours, until the squash is soft.
- Salt and pepper to taste, then serve.

SERVINGS: 6

ARTICHOKE SOUP

Living on the northern California coast, close to Castroville, the self-proclaimed "Artichoke Center of the World," we have an abundance of artichokes and like to do many things with them. Often we just steam them and eat them with a homemade aioli. However, I also love them as a smooth and creamy soup.

INGREDIENTS

1 leek, cleaned and chopped
1 tbsp ghee
3 cloves garlic, crushed
1 sweet potato, peeled and cubed
4 artichokes, trimmed to hearts
1 bay leaf
3 cups chicken stock
2 tbsp fresh lemon juice
6 tomatoes, peeled and chopped
½ tsp dried basil
½ tsp dried oregano
Salt and pepper just before serving

COOKING INSTRUCTIONS

› Sauté the leek in the ghee in a heavy-bottomed pan over medium heat for 5 minutes, until the leek is soft.

› Add the garlic, cook another 3 minutes, then transfer the mixture to the slow cooker.

› Add the rest of the ingredients, starting with sweet potato and then artichokes, and cook on low for 7 hours.

› Discard bay leaf, and puree the soup with an immersion blender or in the food processor.

› Return to the slow cooker for 30 minutes, salt and pepper to taste, then serve.

SERVINGS: 6

PALEO **ONION SOUP**

I vividly remember the first time I tasted French onion soup. It was at a restaurant in Pasadena with my friend's grandparents when I was in high school. I instantly fell in love with the flavor which isn't a surprise because I'm also a huge fan of onion. When I was little, my uncle used to tell me to keep eating them because an onion a day will keep the boys away. Here is my Paleo take on a classic French onion soup.

INGREDIENTS

6 slices bacon, diced
2 leeks, cleaned and sliced
3 large white onions, sliced
2 cloves garlic, crushed
4 cups beef broth
1 bay leaf
2 fresh thyme sprigs
Salt and pepper just before serving

COOKING INSTRUCTIONS

› Fry the bacon in a heavy-bottomed pan over medium heat until just crispy, about 5 minutes, and reserve for garnish.

› Add the leeks and onions to the pan and sauté in the bacon grease for about 5 minutes, until the onions are translucent.

› Add the garlic, cook another 3 minutes, then transfer the mixture to the slow cooker.

› Add the rest of the ingredients and cook on low for 6-8 hours.

› Discard bay leaf and thyme sprigs and stir in the cooked bacon bits.

› Salt and pepper to taste, then serve.

SERVINGS: 6

FENNEL **TOMATO SOUP**

Fennel gives a nice twist to a traditional tomato soup, adding zest to the flavor. This is a great starter for a nice meal.

INGREDIENTS

3 shallots, chopped
1 tbsp ghee
3 cloves garlic, crushed
2 bulbs fennel, chopped
8 cups chopped fresh tomatoes
Juice of 1 lemon
½ tsp dried basil
4 cups chicken broth
Salt and pepper just before serving

COOKING INSTRUCTIONS

- Sauté the shallots in the ghee in a heavy-bottomed pan over medium heat for 5 minutes, until translucent.
- Add the garlic and fennel, cook another 3-5 minutes, until the garlic is fragrant, then transfer the mixture to the slow cooker.
- Add the rest of the ingredients and cook on low for 7 hours.
- Puree the soup with an immersion blender or in your food processor in batches, and return to the slow cooker for another 30 minutes.
- Salt and pepper to taste, then serve.

SERVINGS: 6

SIDES

RED CABBAGE AND APPLE

This is a great way of using up red cabbage in your fridge. We often will get a whole head from our CSA, and it's hard to finish it in a week. This is a delicious side to pair with pork or chicken.

INGREDIENTS

1 small red cabbage, cored and cut into 2-inch squares

2 cooking apples, cored and cut into 1-inch chunks

¼ cup apple cider vinegar

1 onion, diced

¼ cup chicken or veggie stock

2 sprigs of fresh rosemary

2 sprigs of fresh thyme

Salt and pepper just before serving

COOKING INSTRUCTIONS

› Place all ingredients in the slow cooker and cook on low for 3-4 hours.

› Salt and pepper to taste, then serve.

SERVINGS: 6

CAULIFLOWER

Cauliflower is a veggie I grew up with and love. This is a simple way to serve it, and it goes with lots of different main dishes.

INGREDIENTS

1 head of cauliflower
2 cloves garlic, crushed
2 tbsp butter
¼ cup chopped fresh parsley
1 tbsp chopped fresh tarragon
1 cup chicken stock
Salt and pepper just before serving

COOKING INSTRUCTIONS

- Place all ingredients in the slow cooker and cook on low for 3-4 hours, until the cauliflower is tender.
- Salt and pepper to taste, then serve.

SERVINGS: 6

ROASTED BEETS WITH BACON

Beets are another one of my favorite vegetables. They take so long to cook when you roast them that I love the alternative of making them in the slow cooker. On a weekend morning, it only takes me mere minutes to throw them in and by lunchtime have a tasty side. Their sweet flavor is complemented by the smoky flavor of the bacon. And they are great as leftovers, tossed over an arugula salad.

INGREDIENTS

8 medium beets, scrubbed and roots trimmed

SALAD

5 slices bacon, diced
¼ cup minced shallots
2 cloves garlic, crushed
2 tbsp apple cider vinegar
3 tbsp olive oil
2 tbsp finely chopped fresh rosemary
Salt and pepper to taste

COOKING INSTRUCTIONS

- Place beets in the slow cooker, cover and cook on high for 4-5 hours, until the beets are tender.
- While still hot, remove the peels, which should come off easily.
- Dice beets into 1-inch chunks and place in serving dish.
- Cook the bacon in a heavy-bottomed pan over medium heat until crispy, about 6 minutes, then set aside.
- In a bowl, mix the remaining ingredients into a vinaigrette.
- Pour vinaigrette over the beets.
- Top with bacon, salt and pepper to taste, then serve. You can also chill the beets and serve this as a chilled salad.

SERVINGS: 6

TYPE 2 DIABETES PREVENTION AND IMPROVEMENT

Nearly 26 million Americans are currently living with diabetes while another 79 million are in a "pre-diabetic" state, well on their way to the real deal. It's a deadly epidemic and it is not going away. Type 2 Diabetes is largely a "lifestyle disease." Diet, exercise, environment, stress and sleep all play roles in its development, with diet and lack of physical activity being the largest factors. Today's "normal" eating pattern is a giant sugar-and carbohydrate-loaded disaster and it's killing us.

Eating carbohydrate and/or sugar causes the level of glucose in the blood to increase. In response, the pancreas releases insulin to move excess glucose from the blood into muscle and liver cells for storage as glycogen. Glycogen stores are used to fuel the muscles during exercise and/or between meals for energy. Unfortunately, with today's constant supply of carbohydrates/sugar and inactive lifestyle, glycogen stores fill up and close their glucose gates. This triggers the pancreas to make even more insulin so that the muscles take up more glucose. When the muscles don't respond to the signal, the cycle continues. Eventually, the muscles get very good at ignoring insulin altogether and becoming resistant to it. The end result is inability to metabolize/use carbohydrates correctly. Also, remember that inflammation contributes to the development of diabetes, today's diet and lifestyle are both key players here too. The Paleo diet (when implemented correctly) is an effective way to help prevent or even reverse insulin resistance and Type 2 Diabetes.

HERE ARE SOME OF THE WAYS IT WORKS:

A Paleo lifestyle minimizes exposure to inflammation-causing foods, agents and habits.

Paleo eating is largely based on fat and protein, or in cases of the very active, a balance of favorable carbohydrate, protein and fat. A complete "carbo-palooza" or sugar show is next to impossible!

Relying on vegetables and moderate amounts of starchy vegetables and fruit as carbohydrate sources makes it much more difficult to overload glycogen stores when compared to a diet supplying a steady stream of soda and processed snacks.

Smart exercise is a key component in the Paleo way of life. When we exercise we use some of our stored glycogen, making room for more glucose. The muscles have room for glucose and "hear" insulin's signal instead of "resisting" it.

chapter nine

WARM PALEO **DESSERTS**

WE ALL NEED A TREAT EVERY ONCE IN A WHILE, even we Paleo people. Just because some desserts use Paleo ingredients, I don't automatically classify them as healthy. We treat them as treats around here and only eat them occasionally. The slow cooker works great for warm desserts because you can start it when you begin preparing your entrée and by the time you clean up dinner, a warm dessert is waiting. It always impresses guests when we serve warm-spiced pears after dinner.

SLOW-COOKER **BAKED APPLES**

Here's a fantastic fall/winter dessert that might fill the void of an apple pie, if you miss that from your pre-Paleo days.

INGREDIENTS

2 tbsp dried cranberries
2 tbsp honey
½ cup chopped pecans
1 tsp cinnamon
½ tsp nutmeg
2 tbsp coconut oil
8 cooking apples, cored, skin peeled around the top only
½ cup apple cider, apple juice or dry white wine

COOKING INSTRUCTIONS

› In a bowl, mix the cranberries, honey, pecans, half of cinnamon, half of nutmeg and 1 tablespoon coconut oil.

› Fill the middle of the apples with the mixture and carefully place them into the slow cooker.

› Melt the rest of the coconut oil in a pan over medium heat, and add the remaining cinnamon and nutmeg. Combine the mixture with cider, juice or wine, then pour over the apples.

› Cook on high for 2-3 hours, until apples are tender. Let rest for 5 minutes, then serve.

SERVINGS: 8

BERRY RHUBARB MAPLE **CRISP**

I have never been into baking much, but my husband loves berry pies and crisps, so I had to figure out how to make Paleo alternatives to help him stay with the diet. Plus, even Paleo people need a treat every once in a while! Here is a healthier alternative to a traditional berry crisp, but just as tasty! The recipe is a little involved and you need to use your oven at the end to crisp it up.

INGREDIENTS

FILLING

1 tbsp coconut oil
2 cups diced rhubarb, cut into ½-inch pieces
2 cups strawberries
2 cups blackberries
2 tbsp lemon juice
1 tsp cinnamon
¼ tsp powdered ginger
½ cup maple syrup

TOPPING

2 tbsp coconut oil
1 cup almond flour
½ cup pecans
Dash of sea salt
½ tsp nutmeg
2 tbsp maple syrup

COOKING INSTRUCTIONS

› Lightly coat the inside of the slow cooker with coconut oil.

› Mix all the filling ingredients, including the remaining coconut oil, and place in the slow cooker.

› Cook on high for 2 hours or until fruit is tender.

› Preheat the oven to 375 degrees.

› Mix all the topping ingredients, and stir to incorporate. The mixture should resemble crumbles.

› Spread the crumbles over the top of the filling and place stoneware of slow cooker into the oven for 15-20 minutes, until top is crisp. If your stoneware is not oven safe, transfer to an oven-safe dish.

› Let rest for 5 minutes, then serve from the slow-cooker stoneware.

SERVINGS: 6

PALEO **BANANAS COCONUT FOSTER**

Bananas Foster originated in New Orleans during the 1950s. One of the reasons I love this dessert, besides how delicious it is, is my love of all things old. Relaxing at home, listening to Elvis and enjoying a bowl of this dessert is my idea of bliss.

INGREDIENTS

10 bananas, cut into quarters
½ cup chopped walnuts
1 cup coconut flakes
1 tsp cinnamon
¼ cup honey
½ cup coconut oil, melted
2 tsp lemon zest
¼ cup lemon juice
1 tbsp coconut rum
1 tsp vanilla extract
Coconut cream for serving

COOKING INSTRUCTIONS

› Place the bananas in the slow cooker and top with walnuts and coconut flakes.

› Mix together remaining ingredients, except the coconut cream, and pour over the bananas.

› Cook on low for 1½-2 hours, or until bananas are tender, but not mushy.

› Place on plates, pour coconut cream over the top and serve.

SERVINGS: 6

SLOW-COOKED **SPICED PEACHES**

This is one of my new favorites.

INGREDIENTS

8 peaches, peeled and sliced

¼ cup honey

2 tbsp coconut butter

1 tsp cinnamon

½ tsp nutmeg

2 tsp vanilla extract

Dash of sea salt

Coconut cream for serving

COOKING INSTRUCTIONS

› Place peaches in the slow cooker.

› Mix together remaining ingredients, except the coconut cream, and pour over the peaches.

› Cook on high for 1½-2 hours, until peaches are tender.

› Pour coconut cream over the top and serve.

SERVINGS: 6

SLOW-COOKER **APPLESAUCE**

Applesauce is probably the healthiest dessert included here. It still has a lot of sugar so don't eat a lot if you are trying to lose weight. The pears add a little lightness to the flavor.

INGREDIENTS

6 apples, peeled, cored and thinly sliced
2 pears, peeled, cored and thinly sliced
1 tsp cinnamon
1 tsp vanilla extract
2 tbsp honey
Juice from ½ of tangelo or orange
½ tsp ground cloves
½ tsp nutmeg

COOKING INSTRUCTIONS

- Combine all ingredients in the slow cooker.
- Cook on low for 6 hours, stirring occasionally if possible.
- Use an immersion blender or food processor to puree the sauce.

SERVINGS: 6

SIMPLY **SWEET PEARS**

I first made these for my husband on Valentine's Day, and they were delicious and the perfect winter dessert. I usually throw them in before I start cooking dinner and by the time we finish, we have a warm sweet to indulge in. It's important to use Bosc pears because they are firmer than other pears and hold up to the slow cooking. The ginger, while seemingly out of place, is a must in this recipe and gives a terrific and distinctive flavor.

INGREDIENTS

2 tbsp coconut oil, melted
1 tsp grated fresh ginger
¼ tsp cinnamon
⅛ tsp ground cloves
⅛ tsp nutmeg
2 tbsp honey
4 Bosc pears

COOKING INSTRUCTIONS

› Mix all the ingredients, except the pears, in a bowl or large dish.

› Toss the pears in the mixture and coat thoroughly.

› Place pears in the slow cooker and cook on high for 2 hours, until the pears are fork-tender.

SERVINGS: 4

chapter ten

DIRECTIONS ON HOW TO MAKE **DIFFERENT LIQUIDS FOR EXCEPTIONAL SLOW COOKING**

WE TRY TO AVOID USING CANNED FOODS AS MUCH AS POSSIBLE, as they often have BPA and other chemicals that can leach into the contents. In the case of coconut milk, there are often additives and gums in the canned version. It is surprisingly easy and more nutritious to make your own slow-cooker liquids!

HOMEMADE **COCONUT MILK**

We try to limit our use of canned coconut milk. The good thing is you can find some BPA-free brands, but most of them have additional ingredients such as guar gum. A brand of packaged coconut milk many people prefer is Aroy-D, as the only ingredients are coconuts and water and the tetra-pak is BPA free. I still think the healthiest option is to make it yourself!

There are various ways to make coconut milk. Two options are to make it from desiccated coconuts or from fresh coconuts, the latter taking a fair amount of work.

OPTION 1: USING DESSICATED COCONUTS

INGREDIENTS

8-oz package of desiccated coconut

3 cups boiling water

COOKING INSTRUCTIONS

- Place the coconut and water in a blender for about 45 seconds.
- Line a strainer with 2 layers of cheesecloth.
- Pour the contents of the blender through the strainer into a large bowl.
- Pull the edges of the cheesecloth together and squeeze the remainder of the coconut milk out.
- Refrigerate the coconut milk and use within 1-2 days.

MAKES: 3 cups

OPTION 2: FRESH COCONUTS

INGREDIENTS

Meat from 1 coconut, shell removed and meat grated

2 cups hot to boiling water

COOKING INSTRUCTIONS

› Place the coconut and water in a blender or food processor, preferably a powerful one, and blend until liquid.

› Line a strainer with 2 layers of cheesecloth.

› Pour the contents of the blender through the strainer into a large bowl.

› Pull the edges of the cheesecloth together and squeeze the remainder of the coconut milk.

› Refrigerate the coconut milk and use within 1-2 days.

MAKES: 2 cups

BROTH

INGREDIENTS

3 lbs beef or chicken bones
1 medium onion, quartered
2 carrots, cut into chunks
2 stalks celery, with leaves, cut into chunks
2 bay leaves
3 cloves garlic, peeled
½ tsp dried rosemary
½ tsp dried marjoram
½ tsp dried thyme
½ tsp dried basil
1 tsp dried parsley
1 tbsp whole peppercorns
8-12 cups filtered water
2 tbsp apple cider vinegar
Juice of 1 lemon

COOKING INSTRUCTIONS

› Place all the ingredients in the slow cooker and cook on low for 8 hours (or up to 24 hours).

› Skim foam or excess oil from the top.

› Remove all vegetables and bones, and put broth through a strainer.

› Refrigerate or freeze for later use.

MAKES: 8-12 cups

BLANCHING **TOMATOES**

This is a great and easy way to peel tomatoes but is not a slow-cooker recipe.

COOKING INSTRUCTIONS

› Boil about 4 quarts of water.

› Set up a cold bath of water in a large bowl with some ice cubes.

› Cut an "X" in the bottom of each tomato (up to 8 tomatoes at a time), drop in the boiling water carefully and cook for 1 minute.

› Remove a few tomatoes at a time and dunk in the cold bath.

› The skin should now easily peel off by hand.

› Trim the tomato top and then follow the recipe directions.

THE LOST ART OF HOMEMADE BROTH

I clearly remember when my practitioner asked me to include homemade stock in my daily diet. I felt intimidated; it seemed like such a daunting task. Although I had been cooking for quite some time, every time a recipe called for stock or broth, I would buy the "healthiest, most organic" option I could find. Once I made broth and saw how incredibly easy it actually was, and when I learned of all the health benefits, I could not believe this is something that most of us no longer do regularly. Now, there is always broth in our freezer!

I consider homemade broth as my secret ingredient. I could not believe the difference in recipes that I once made with store-bought broth. These meals are much richer and more flavorful with homemade broth.

Stock and broths are used in almost all traditional cuisines. Even Americans made stock regularly for a long time, chances are some of our mothers and most of our grandmothers are very familiar with this practice. Since most of us are purchasing muscle meats and boneless chicken breasts, we don't usually have bones lying around to make stock.

Bone broth is one of the most nutrient-dense foods that we can consume. It is rich in collagen, gelatin, amino acids and many minerals. The calcium in bone broth is in a form that is very easy for the body to absorb and digest. Research and observation of traditional cultures have taught us that gelatin has many benefits including improving digestion and soothing the GI Tract. In addition, it has been found to build strong cartilage and bones and it has benefits for the skin, immune system and heart. It is a true superfood! That's why Grandma always made us soup when we felt under the weather!

Unfortunately, store-bought broth does not offer these same benefits, as it is usually not made with real gelatin, but uses emulsifiers instead, and many use artificial flavors. Luckily, homemade broth is very easy to make. I have included a recipe for you. Basically, you can add 3 to 4 lbs of high-quality bones to a slow cooker, fill it up with approximately 10 cups of filtered water, add any vegetable/herb scraps that you might have. And add a couple of tablespoons of vinegar, as the vinegar helps extract more nutrients from the bones. Cook on low for 8 hours to overnight.

Fresh broth will keep in the refrigerator for several days and it can be frozen for a very long time. If making broth really does not appeal to you, the best alternative is purchasing homemade broth from US Wellness Meats at www.grasslandbeef.com!

HEALTH BENEFITS OF COLLAGEN

Collagen is a protein key to the formation and maintenance of tendons, ligaments, muscles, cartilage, hair and nails. With age, the amount of collagen the body makes decreases, so collagen supplementation/consumption may help reduce the signs of aging. Collagen also plays a role in improving circulation by strengthening blood vessels and increasing their elasticity. Additionally, collagen functions to promote healing and the repair and synthesis of connective tissue. There are also implications that collagen may be helpful in relieving arthritis due to its role in the joints and the tissues surrounding them.

The best sources of collagen include bones, skin and cartilage, most of what you make broth from. A side note that most studies on the health benefits of collagen have been based on use of supplements rather than food forms, so dosage levels are likely much higher than the amounts consumed in a healthy Paleo diet.

RECIPE **INDEX**

INDEX

R

S

ARSY'S STORY

LEVERAGING NUTRITION TO ACHIEVE HEALTH AND WELLNESS was a concept that I was always drawn to. In my journey to find optimal health, I made many nutrition decisions that actually had the opposite effect. This was a direct result of the massive amount of inaccurate information in the mainstream and the lack of knowledge that not all, but many medical professionals have about the effects of nutrition on health.

I come from a family with a wide array of lifestyle-triggered health conditions—type 2 diabetes, obesity, high blood pressure, and the list goes on. As a teen, I had an instinct that my family's health problems were directly linked to diet and lifestyle. However, I didn't know enough about nutrition to really make sense out of it. I did know that I didn't want to end up unhealthy, overweight or sick. In my early efforts to be healthy I turned to vegetarianism. At 16, I knew little about nutrition and had been bombarded with messages that meat is bad, fat is bad, and it all causes heart disease. With all this misinformation I converted to a much less healthy diet than the Middle-Eastern/Mediterranean one I was raised on. So for the next nine years, I lived off bagels, pasta, sandwiches, beans, salads, some veggies, tofu and lots and lots of pre-packaged, processed, gluten-filled, soy products like fake chicken. After a few years of eating this way, I felt incredibly lethargic and experienced constant headaches. I saw a multitude of doctors and none of them were able to solve my health issues, nor were they able to connect how I felt to how I was eating. I was told quite the opposite. My diet was very healthy, they said. Trusting their authority, I continued to microwave my Morningstar meals and my health continued to plummet through my 20s.

When I started CrossFit many years ago, I was introduced to the Paleo diet and became headache-free for the first time in years. I felt full of energy. Also, the constant bloating that I experienced, the one that caused me to look pregnant in high school when I only weighed

98 pounds also disappeared. My problem with constant overeating also vanished. I used to eat until I was in pain, almost nightly. I instantly noticed that didn't happen on a Paleo diet. I was satiated and didn't have the urge to keep eating.

Although the Paleo Diet helped me tremendously, I was still experiencing headaches and was fatigued more often than I was comfortable with. After working with an amazing practioner, Chris Kresser, author of the introduction to this book, I discovered I also had anemia caused by a B12 deficiency and a low performing thyroid, which I had suspected for years, but conventional doctors never gave me the proper tests. Although I was consuming B12 in the form of animal protein, I was not absorbing it. Along with some supplements and modifications to my diet, we were able to cure my conditions. From this process, I learned that it was not only important to reduce or eliminate food toxins, it is also essential to include nutrient-dense foods in any diet such as homemade bone broths, fermented foods and healthy fats.

As a result of feeling better—feeling normal again as I like to call it—I was able to focus on my passions and interests. Paleo eating allowed me to rekindle my love of cooking, which I had given up during my vegetarian phase. Now I regularly enjoy shopping and searching for fresh, organic, grass-fed ingredients to create delicious meals for my family. I wanted to share the recipes that made me feel so good and weren't hard to do. I hope they work for you.

ABOUT THE **AUTHORS**

ARSY VARTANIAN has been interested in the connection between health and nutrition since she was a teen. She is the classic convert whose story underscores the power of the Paleo diet. She started as a vegetarian to seek optimal health, but after a couple of years she felt lethargic and was experiencing constant headaches. She saw a multitude of doctors, and none of them were able to solve her health issues. It wasn't until she started Crossfit that she discovered the Paleo diet. Magically she was headache free for the first time in years, and felt full of energy. It so successfully transformed her personal health, she has become a Paleo promoter and shares recipes on her popular blog, rubiesandradishes.com. This book contains original recipes plus a handful of favorites from her blog.

AMY KUBAL is a Registered and Licensed Dietitian specializing in the Paleo diet and performance nutrition. She is the consulting dietitian for Robb Wolf and the director of Wolf's Paleo RD Network. Additionally she is the nutrition guru for the Whole9, and Joe Friel's Training Bible coaching. She works with a broad range of performance focused clients made up of Olympic athletes, IronMan triathletes, professional bikers, marathoners, CrossFit games competitors, MMA fighters, Kettlebell masters, and everyday athletes. She contributed the nutrition information. More information on Amy can be found at http://robbwolf.com/about/team/amy-kubal/.

CHRIS KRESSER is a Paleo community leader and functional medicine practitioner. His blog, ChrisKresser.com, is one of the most popular on the topic. Arsy was one of his clients. He can be found at www.chriskresser.com.